A Note to the Reader...

This book was written in **2002** under the title "_An Old Helicopter Pilot Remembers Vietnam_" as a legacy to my children, and was not originally intended for distribution to the general public.

But, word got around, and fam" ... ds begin asking for a copy. These ... detailed below:

Edition History—

2003 The _1st Edition_ was printed on a laser printer and bound by a spiral 'comb'. Ten copies were distributed between my four children, with a few spare copies for myself.

2004 The _2nd Edition_ was published on CD's as requests were received. Some additional anecdotes were included.

2005 The _3rd Edition_ was hand published by me in book form in only 6 copies. A few minor changes were made to correct typos, etc. Again, the copies were distributed between the four children, with a few spare copies for me.

2007 The _4th Edition_ was made available in eBook form. This was the first Edition designed for public consumption. Both a title change and some minor editing were accomplished. Since this was to be a "public" project and there was difficulty in locating individuals named in earlier Editions, all personal names were eliminated.

2008 The _5th Edition_ was commercially published in book form. Along with deleting family names, a series of changes were made including the addition of some new anecdotal material and a reformatting to realign book pages.

2010 This _6th Edition_ is published with reformatted pictures to improve their quality. Minor text changes were made.

I sincerely hope you will be able to "sit back and enjoy" as you read about how an Old Helicopter Pilot remembers Vietnam in "_Vietnam Air Rescues_"

Dave Richardson

*"May God always
ride with you as
He has ridden with me."*

Jolly Green '67 - '68

"Up in the air, depending on prayer"

By Dave Richardson

I would like to thank the following people:
- My beloved wife, <u>Kaye</u>, who has offered continuous support and encouragement
- My four sons—
  <u>Craig</u>, for being the sparkplug without which this book would not be in existence;
  <u>David</u> and <u>Mark</u>, for invaluable technical assistance;
  <u>Eric</u>, for his encouragement and locating my editor
- <u>Debbie Hill</u>, my editor, who added the final polish.

THAT OTHERS MAY LIVE

RESCUE

JOLLY GREEN

Introduction

Introduction

Winter – 2002

To my four sons, David, Craig, Eric and Mark—

I am writing this to you boys, more than 30 years after the fact, due primarily to the encouragement (badgering) of Craig. The catalyst was me receiving an account of the experiences of the survivor of my final rescue in June, 1968. I wrote a counterpoint to his narrative and found I was enthused about the project.

As a Christian, when I departed for Vietnam, I felt in my heart, that God was assuring me I would return. Not necessarily in one piece or without a stint as a POW, but I felt assured that I _would_ return. This gave me a calmness and inner peace that was not available to all of my squadron mates. During my tour, I made several rescues, and although some of the missions were quite difficult, I could always feel the hand of God on me. This gave me a confidence that the risks were worthwhile.

Here, in this document, are my remembrances of Vietnam . . .

Love, **Dad**

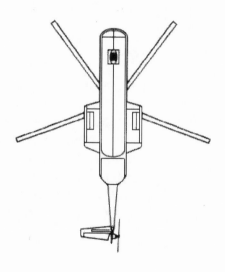

Table of Contents

Jolly Greens lined up on Ramp

Table of Contents

6th Edition – 2010

Survivors' View of Helicopter

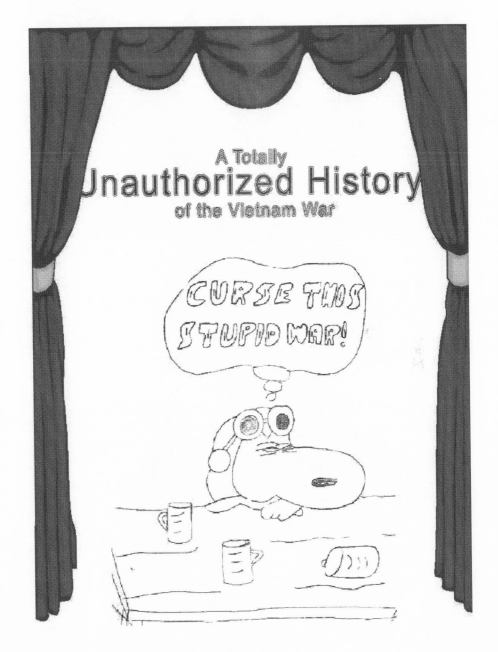

"Jolly Green" Himself

A Totally Unauthorized History of the Vietnam War

With all the years that have gone by, few remember the aching division of our country that was caused by the Vietnam War. The questions at the time were

1 How did we get into it?
2 What are we doing there?
3 How do we get out of it?

In this section, I will attempt to give you my perspective on the answers to those questions.

I must caution you that, while all that I will tell you is true, it is also from my own point of view. Please understand that 'political correctness' may make these points of view unpopular today. With that little caveat, I will attempt a (somewhat) short history of the Vietnam War.

To truly understand what we call the Vietnam War, both a history and geography lesson are in order. What was loosely called Southeast Asia (hence the acronym 'SEA' heard so much during the war period) consisted primarily of 5 countries: These were Cambodia, Thailand, Laos, and North and South Vietnam.

If your geography is a little "sketchy", it might be helpful to consult the map on the next page.

Southeast Asia Map

Of the 5 countries named, only Thailand (formerly known as Siam) had a true history of independence. This is of some importance in the scope of things.

The rest of the countries had a long history of subjugation by one power or another. For over a hundred years, this area, with the exception of Thailand, had been known as '*French Indo-China*' and was dominated and ruled by the French.

Desiring the areas' strategic materials, the Japanese invaded and conquered the entire region during the Second World War. In fact, the first base I was assigned to (Udorn Royal Thai Air Base), on the Laotian border, was an old Japanese airfield dating to World War 2. I saw some of the old hangers and huts, although we couldn't enter the complex due to mines and unexploded ordinance.

During World War 2, both the French and the Americans provided arms and encouraged the inhabitants to fight the Japanese. At the end of the war, the French attempted to reclaim their former colonies. This, however, did not sit too well with the locals who thought they had been promised independence if they would fight the Japanese (in fact, they had been promised exactly that!). The locals went from fighting the Japanese one day to fighting the returning French the next. This quiet little war went on for several years.

The United States, having its own adventure in a place called Korea, resisted the idea of helping the French, who used the famed French Foreign Legion in their attempt to force the area back into colonial status. Finally, in the 1950's, the French Foreign Legion was astonishingly defeated at a place called Dien Bien Phu. The French were shocked at this setback and eventually withdrew from the region.

The country of Vietnam was created out of this chaos and power vacuum. The 1950's and 1960's were times of great expansion for communism as they began to infiltrate and undermine the fledgling governments of the region. First to fall was Laos, which, despite calls for help, the United States refused to assist.

With the fall of Laos, it was the United States' turn to be shocked. Partly in response to these events, the United States formed the _Southeast Asia Treaty Organization_ (SEATO), which included the various nations, in the area and, significantly, the United States.

SEATO was supposed to halt communism in Southeast Asia its tracks. The general idea was that if any member nation were attacked, the others would come to its assistance. Obviously, the United States was _not_ depending on military help from Vietnam, but it did provide a face-saving measure for the Vietnamese.

Instant fighting broke out throughout all of Vietnam. Finally, the United Nations stepped in and divided the nation in half—the northern part becoming North Vietnam and the southern part South Vietnam.

A truce was called for, during which time the people were to vote with their feet. The choice was go north for communism; south for democracy. Many of the people in the north were no fools. They began heading south as fast as their feet would carry them. Thus began a time of great cruelty, with the communist's hideously maiming and murdering people who refused to agree with them.

A Dr. Dooley was in Vietnam during this time, attempting to bring medical aid to the unfortunates who were caught in the middle. His book, _The Night They Burned the Mountain_, detailed some of the brutal treatment inflicted upon innocents who attempted to escape. (One example mentioned in the book: the communists would hold a person down and drive a 10", or so, bamboo splinter into each ear canal, then release them and tell them they could now walk to the south. Of course, their sense of balance was destroyed, and they would blunder around in circles, constantly falling down, which provided a source of amusement to the communists. After a time, the ear canals would become infected and the person would die in great agony.)

Dooley's book, along with other documented accounts of atrocities caused great revulsion in the West.

Finally, a 'democratic' government was established in the south. Right away there was a problem. The situation was roughly analogous to that in the United States at the outbreak of our Civil War. The northern part of Vietnam, which was now communist, contained virtually all the industry and trained bureaucrats, while the south was basically agrarian, with few or no governmental skills among the populace. Worse yet, the common peasants who had lived in the south all their lives had never known freedom and scarcely knew or cared which government held power. All they wanted was to be left alone.

The government in the south became increasingly corrupt as they taxed the peasants without mercy while offering them little or nothing in return. The communists began slyly infiltrating cadres into the south who questioned the validity of the democratic government, while making extravagant promises for communism. Some of the people fell for this propaganda. Those who did not were murdered along with their families. Thus did the infamous Viet Cong's influence grow.

Then the so-called "*Cuban Missile Crisis*" occurred in the early 1960's. This pitted a young, inexperienced American president (John F. Kennedy) against the Russian monolith. To encourage the Russians to back down in Cuba, the United States made some sweeping concessions of its own, affecting the city of Berlin and American bases in Turkey. In the aftermath, it was widely felt that the Americans had come off second best.

Casting about for an easy political way to 'save face', Kennedy created the Green Berets and decided to answer the increasingly pitiful cries for help from the South Vietnamese government. He authorized increased financial aid to South Vietnam along with American military help in the form of "advisors" to train the woefully inept South Vietnamese military.

It is now alleged that by the time of his assassination, Kennedy realized we were being drawn into a quagmire and was quietly making plans to pull U.S. troops out. Whether or not that is true, he was killed before anything came of it and the new president, Johnson, was left with the option of retreating in humiliation or increasing our level of assistance. We were duty bound by the SEATO treaty to come to the aid of the South Vietnamese. Therefore, the entire effort was cast as a humanitarian one.

Back in the U.S., liberal leaders (who would later encourage anti-war activities at home) demanded the United States use its formidable power to intervene. Apparently it never occurred to them that someone was bound to get hurt during a war. However, when increasing numbers of Americans began coming home in caskets or maimed, and appalling stories of Vietnamese deaths became public, these same people began to decry the very military they had demanded be sent.

It is also important to realize that, during this time, Americans, in general, were terrified of communist expansion. Most Americans fervently believed in the so-called '*Domino Effect*', which taught that if South Vietnam fell, the entire region (with its strategic resources) would follow.

In addition, many Americans, especially the military, had contempt for the military abilities of the Vietnamese, who they considered 'inferior' militarily. (I say this was the prevalent attitude. I doubt you could find it expressed so pointedly in print elsewhere.) America poured tons of financial and military aid into South Vietnam, whose successive governments remained hopelessly corrupt.

When it was widely (and correctly) reported that the South Vietnamese units were dropping their weapons and running at the first sight of the enemy, the decision was made to allow the American "advisors" to accompany the South Vietnamese into the field. It was hoped that this would stiffen the resolve of the South Vietnamese. This only led to the beginning of American casualties. There was an immediate uproar in the States to either bring the 'boys' home or send fighting troops.

Ostensibly in response to official requests through SEATO and due to several events including the famous _Gulf of Tonkin_ incident (which many now claim was fabricated), the United States began sending increasingly large numbers of combat forces to fight in Vietnam. At first, the Americans fought alongside the South Vietnamese. Gradually, the Americans took over the brunt of the fighting, aided by other countries such as Australia and South Korea, who also sent troops.

From the beginning, the American war effort was hopelessly bungled. If the truth were known, America had no strategic interest in the region. In fact, most Americans had never heard of the place until their sons or husbands were sent there to fight. Instead of mobilizing the American populace to support the war, the government termed the effort a 'conflict' and downplayed both its seriousness and the possible consequences. No declaration of war was sought and what was termed a 'guns and butter' economy (meaning no shortages or rationing; a complete peacetime atmosphere at home with the war conveniently tucked half a world away) was practiced. American forces were rotated into and out of Vietnam on a calendar basis.

American forces fought under impossible '_Rules of Engagement_'. These prohibited firing at the enemy until he fired at you, thus requiring the soldier to risk his life on the premise that the enemy was a bad shot. In addition, territory was never held, only secured. Americans would 'take' or 'sanitize' an area, incurring causalities, only to abandon it and return to their fortified bases. The predictable result was that often those same troops would be called upon to fight for the same area a few days or weeks later, only to abandon it once again. Jungle fighting neutralized America's famed technological prowess. A typical 'battle' was a small American patrol being ambushed along a jungle trail. Often, due to the dense vegetation, the enemy was never seen.

In Vietnam, Communist sympathizers were everywhere. Walk past the peasant tending his rice paddy and he might shoot you in the back. Women and children would deliver booby-trapped articles to the unwary Americans. The tall, foreign-appearing Americans stood out, while the communists blended into the general populace.

Soldiers began living for their "DEROS"; their *Date of Estimated Return from Over Seas*. With the continuous calendar rotation, units were always short of experienced leaders and men and thus forced to learn the basic lessons of jungle combat over and over again.

The communists, alas, were not stupid. They correctly realized they stood no chance in open combat against American units. Therefore, they stayed with small unit 'guerilla' activities using primitive ambushes and booby-traps such as the infamous "*Punji sticks*" (pointed stakes, smeared with excrement and hidden along the side of trails); which were designed to inflict causalities, rather than deaths among American troops. The theory was that if you kill an American, you have taken one soldier out of the fighting, but if you wound an American, you take out up to 5 soldiers who must transport and care for the wounded man.

In spite of all this, the Americans *were* effective. In response, regular North Vietnamese troops began arriving in South Vietnam in force to supplant the Viet Cong irregulars. Constant re-supply was accomplished along the so-called '*Ho Chi Minh Trail*'; actually a series of primitive roads and trails leading from North Vietnam (increasingly through Laos) into South Vietnam. The American solution was to bomb first the trails, then the staging and supply points in North Vietnam. Initially, only fighter aircraft were used, but finally, the mighty B-52 bombers began flying sorties into North Vietnam.

Sighting enemy troops moving on foot or bicycles through the triple-layer canopy of dense jungle proved nearly impossible. The same _Rules of Engagement_ applied to the aircraft crews as the ground soldiers. Extreme, often excessive, care was used to avoid civilian targets. Since our current 'smart' bombs were in their infancy, the unguided iron bombs used had a fair amount of inaccuracy. This caused some targets to remain off-limits during the course of the war. Additionally, vast areas of North Vietnam that were close to the border of China were also declared off-limits.

A massive series of raids took place over the north. Target lists were drawn up, not by the military, but by a civilian bureaucracy thousands of miles away in Washington D.C. which often had little or no appreciation of the military situation. Aircraft began to be lost to the rather sophisticated anti-aircraft defenses supplied by Russia; those pilots who could not be rescued became POW's (prisoners' of war).

Just about the time American crews became familiar with the location of the surface-to-air (SAM) missile sites, a bombing halt would be called in the futile hope the North Vietnamese would capitulate. During the lull, those SAM sites would be relocated. Then, new raids would be ordered; increasing numbers of planes would be lost until the elusive SAM sites were re-identified in their new locations.

At home, everything related to the war was a mess. Americans could not understand why a "vastly inferior" third-world country was withstanding the vaunted American war machine. With no clear-cut goals, questions began to be raised. Why was America involved in Vietnam? If we were there to rescue a legitimate democratic government, why did the people we were trying to help seem not to care?

The American government could not, or would not, produce a satisfactory response. Instead, numerous deadlines for bringing the troops home were set and ignored. The standard of how well the war was progressing became the number of enemy dead for each action. This was called the '_body count_'. Invariably, inflated body counts were produced as a means of justifying the prolongation of the war.

The populace began to doubt its own leaders, questioning why Americans had to die in a distant foreign country of such little concern to them. At the same time, the dreaded draft began sucking away constantly increasing numbers of young men, returning too many of them in body bags or horribly mutilated.

Those who were smart or rich enough to stay in college were exempt from service. Some of those who did not have, or could not fake, physical or educational exemptions simply took the cowards way out and fled the country. Increasingly the draftees sent to Vietnam were seen to be the poor or disadvantaged.

Communist sympathizers and so-called "bleeding hearts" began a backlash of active dissent. Draft records were destroyed; anti-war rallies were staged; returning servicemen who had answered their country's call were spit upon in the streets and called "_Baby-Killers_". It was difficult for the returning servicemen to understand how a country could ask you to serve and then berate you when you fulfilled that request. Everyone seemed to be at each other's throats.

Peace talks were started, halted, and then started again. At one time, several months were spent haggling over the shape of the negotiating table! Finally, American resolve gave way and, for the first time in history, America abandoned an ally during hostilities and left the field.

The result was predictable. Within a disconcertedly short time South Vietnam was overrun and disappeared as an entity. Native people who had taken the American side, believing America's promises of support and assistance were left to die.

At home, both sides nursed bitter grievances. It appeared all the death, injury and destruction had been for nothing. America had 'lost' a war and was nearly torn apart. To this day, resentments simmer. Veterans remember 'Hanoi Jane' Fonda giving aid and comfort to an enemy while Americans were dying at the hands of that same enemy. Anti-war protestors remember the unfortunate Kent State shooting by an unprepared National Guard.

Worst of all, many Americans lost all hope and confidence in their government, which had lied to them so often during the war years. A spirit of antagonism toward authority settled over the country. Coincidently or not, drug abuse became rampant and cynicism reigned. What had started as a noble desire to answer a call to assist a needy people had degenerated into bitterness and a loss of esteem from which America is just now emerging.

The disillusioned troops who returned home to jeers and derision, rather than open arms and congratulations, often faced their critics with two rallying cries:

"If you weren't there, shut your mouth." and

"When I die I know I will go to heaven, because I've spent my time in hell."

This is my view of the history of the Vietnam War. Once again, I need to caution you that others may, and do, have a differing perspective. Everyone who fought in Vietnam saw the war differently.

A-1E Skyraider

In the
Beginning

Ready for takeoff

In the Beginning

Note: There are quite a few military acronyms used throughout this book. If you come upon one that you are not familiar with, feel free to consult the **_Jargon_** section at the end of this book.

A few statistics might be in order:

My rank when I went to SEA (South East Asia) was Captain (O4).

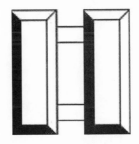

I held a straight-wing pilot's rating.

I was assigned to Detachment One of the 37th Air Rescue Squadron (or Aerospace Rescue and Recovery Squadron, as changed to by the Air Force). Although classified as a Detachment, we functioned as a separate Squadron, with our own Squadron Commander.

I flew 107 combat missions, totaling about 650 hours of combat time. (I believe my records now show about 450 hours. I did not discover this error until several years later, when I was undergoing a records review. I was told that persons unknown had made an 'administrative adjustment' to my records. No explanation was given and I did not have any hard copies to prove my case.)

I rescued 9 people on 7 pickups and flew "High" bird on another three pickups that rescued an additional four people.

In the medals category, I received the following decorations:

| Silver Star | Distinguished Flying Cross (3) | Air Medal (4) | Vietnamese Cross of Gallantry | Vietnam Service Medal | Vietnam Campaign Medal |

When consulting my 'flak' (enemy anti-aircraft gun) map while writing up these experiences, I was surprised and pleased to find that I had recorded the particulars of each rescue on the back of the map. I also discovered an entry for a rescue I had forgotten!

My intent in this section is to give some common general background before telling the story of the rescues.

We were called the **_Jolly Green Giants_**. Our call sign was **_Jolly Green_** or, simply, **_Jolly_**. How this name, which pre-dated my arrival, came about, I am not certain. Evidently, someone likened our large, green and sand colored helicopters to the then popular television commercials for the Jolly Green Giant Company, which heavily advertised their vegetables with the slogan, "Welcome to the land of the Jolly (Ho! Ho! Ho!) Green Giant!"

Jolly Green Patch

Originally I was to be assigned to a third rescue squadron, which was forming in the highlands of Vietnam, Quang Tri, I believe. But, when I arrived in Saigon, the idea of a third rescue squadron had been scrapped. So, I spent a few days waiting while the powers that be pondered whether to keep me in Vietnam or send me to Thailand. The decision was finally Thailand, and I was sent to _Udorn RTAB_, just across the river from communist-controlled Laos.

A short time into my tour, our unit was moved further south and inland to _Nakon Phanom RTAB_, somewhat affectionately known as "Naked Fanny" or, simply "NKP".

Udorn RTAB – My First Base

Nakon Phanom RTAFB - My Second Base

The reason for our move was that a larger and more powerful helicopter, the HH-53, had arrived. There was some discussion as to what their call sign would be. Originally they declined to assume our name, Jolly Green, and toyed with things like BUFF, for _Big Ugly Fat Fellow_ (only it wasn't 'fellow'!). This name, however, was usurped by the B-52's, so they came to be known as "**_Super Jolly's_**".

We, of course, retaliated by advising people, "Don't accept substitutes! Insist on the original Jolly Green".

DON'T ACCEPT SUBSTITUTES
INSIST ON THE ORGINAL

JOLLY GREENS

DET 1   37 ARRS

The helicopter we flew, the HH-3E was also big—too big. It made an easy target. On the plus side, it had good range and was, for a helicopter, very rugged. It was powered by two jet engines and had a boat hull, which allowed it to be landed in the open water of lakes or oceans. Due to the boat design, it had retractable landing gear, which was unusual for a helicopter.

The landing gear was of the tricycle type, with the nose gear folding up into the body and each side gear retracting into boxes affixed to the side of the helicopter called "sponsons", which also served to prevent the helicopter from rolling over while floating on the water.

The floor of the cargo area was the fuel tank, which wasn't such a good feature for combat purposes. The helicopter had a ramp in the rear, which could be lowered. The interior was large enough that two jeeps could be driven, end-to-end, inside the cargo area.

HH-3E Jolly Green

There was a large sliding door on the right side, with two small windows aft in the side of the fuselage. On the left side were three small windows.

The rescue hoist was permanently affixed above the cabin door. Entrance to the cockpit was by the cabin door and then a right turn through a short passage.

We had roughly four hours flying time with full fuel. Each "sponson" was equipped with an F-100 drop tank, which could be jettisoned from the cockpit. This gave us an extra two hours of flight time for a total of approximately six hours.

In addition, we had a retractable in-flight refueling probe, which allowed us to refuel from specially equipped C-130 aircraft.

As was usual with helicopters, the HH-3E was short on power. All non-essential equipment had been removed. For this reason, we flew off the drops first. Just before going into a hover, the drop tanks, which were quite heavy even when empty, were jettisoned.

Each helicopter carried four crewmembers: two Officers and two Enlisted men. The pilot-in-command was called the RCC (**_Rescue Crew Commander_**). His job was to fly the helicopter, be in command of the crew, and take charge as "**_On-Scene Commander_**" when the A-1 support fighters (call sign "**_Sandy_**") felt they had eliminated as many of the enemy guns as they could. The second pilot was known simply as the **_Co-Pilot_**. He was to perform any duties delegated to him by the RCC.

The other two crew members were the **_Flight Mechanic_** who did triple duty as Crew Chief, right gunner and hoist operator; and the **_PJ_** ("Parajumper") who also did triple duty as medic, left gunner and the person who rode the hoist to the ground if the situation warranted.

Originally, we flew unarmed. The policy was that we were there to save lives, not take them.

We get our Guns

After I had been in country a short time, each helicopter was fitted with two M-60 machine guns. The one on the right was fired from the door by the Flight Mechanic and had to be swung aside during a pickup. The other gun was fired by the PJ through the left forward window which was permanently removed.

At first, I considered the guns useless; the gun on the right had to be folded aside and was inoperative during a rescue, and the PJ, who manned the left gun, could be called upon to ride the hoist down to attend to a wounded survivor. But, as you will see, I did come to appreciate them.

We had bases, run by the CIA in enemy-controlled Laos. Since no American servicemen were officially in Laos, we flew without national insignia on the aircraft or any kind of rank or identification on our uniforms.

Jolly Green in flight - Note the absence of national insignia

Actually, we did have metal plates with national insignia on them for the U.S. and all surrounding countries, which could be slid into slots on the outside of the fuselage. Theoretically, we were supposed to insert the U.S. ones when we scrambled for a rescue. I do not know of anyone who bothered.

During the time I was there, I (as well as every other RCC) had a $100,000 bounty on my head for anyone who could deliver my body, dead or alive, to the North Vietnamese.

We wore little camouflaged "Derby" hats instead of a flight cap. This total lack of identification meant that the Geneva Convention did not apply to us and any Jolly Green crewmember who was captured was subject to be immediately shot as a spy.

**Me with Derby Hat (Note the Leopard skin!)
being congratulated after a Pickup**

Our schedule was roughly as follows:

- Three days, two nights locked up in the Alert Hut (a room with sleeping quarters near the helicopter parking area) at home base, followed by a day off.
- Three days, two nights up "North", followed by a day or so off.
- A day of Squadron duty (basically paperwork or additional duty assignments). For instance, I was the OIC (Officer-in-charge) of the Flight Mechanics, and was thus tasked with their administrative supervision.
- Then back to the Alert Hut for another cycle.

Although at times the process varied, it pretty much followed this pattern.

Alert Facility at NKP

Here I Am – Ready to go on my 1st Mission

On our "Northern" alerts, we used two sites: a ***Daytime Site*** and a ***Nighttime Site***. We would take-off each day, before first light, so as to be at the Daytime Site as the sun came up. There was no tower and no one spoke English anyway, so when we approached, we would buzz the strip a few times to see if we could draw any ground fire. If we did, which happened occasionally, we would go to an alternate site, otherwise, we would assume the site was still ours and land.

There were a few times when I had to go to an alternate site. The enemy never seemed to figure out that if they would just hold their fire until we got on the ground, they would have us. But, they always started firing enthusiastically when we were still about a mile or so out.

Alternate Lima Site

41

Usually, we could use our main Daytime Site up 'North'. It was our northernmost one, called **_Lima 36_**, and was near the northeastern Laos/North Vietnamese border, a few miles southwest of Hanoi. It was little more than a short, bulldozed dirt strip, guarded by a 'fortress' manned by tribesmen. The strip, or runway, was too short to accommodate any but light aircraft and helicopters, so our support fighters (A-1's) remained in Thailand until the scramble order came.

Lima 36 – The Daytime Site

HH-3E Landing at Lima 36

On alert at Lima 36

The runway at Lima 36 ended in a drop off of about 40 feet, which contained the wrecks of several fixed-wing aircraft that had not made it.

Debris and unexploded shells off end of runway

This guy had a bad day

This one almost made it. A little battle damage.

Note the insignia

The CIA would drop off stacks of 50-gallon fuel drums, which we used for refueling. We would stand each barrel on end, knock a hole in it, and stick a hose down inside. We had a gas powered pump which would transfer the fuel from the drum to the aircraft.

Once the drum was empty, we had no further use for it, so we would give it to the tribesmen, who would chop the ends off, chisel down the side and flatten it out. They used them as housing material for the fortress that stood on a small rise. The noise of them hammering on the barrels all day long was deafening.

Lima 36 refueling area

Our quarters at the Daytime Site consisted of a small, wooden hut, with four sets of top and bottom bunks and a battery-powered FM radio. There were no windows, just 4 walls and a single door.

Alert Hut at Lima 36

We would spend the entire day, from sunrise to just before sunset, in the hut. We had to stay inside as much as possible, because the jungle's edge was only a few hundred yards away and the enemy would sometimes sneak down and take potshots at us.

Praise the Lord, they never seemed to figure out that they could just shoot through the thin plywood walls and get us all. When they became bothersome, we would 'sic' the tribesmen on them.

Surrounding our hut on three sides was an area covered by waist-high grass. It was filled with unexploded shells and ammunition that would (and did) go off if disturbed.

View of grassy area with jungle in background

Sometimes, we would hear an explosion outside. "Guess another one tried to sneak up on us," we would say.

Debris and unexploded shells near Alert Hut

Me, in doorway of Alert Hut

We left our 'birds' "cocked" on alert status. All we had to do was jump inside and punch the start button as the Flight Mechanic pulled the chocks. Everything else was set up. I held the unofficial Squadron record. I could be airborne in 27 seconds from the time we heard the scramble call on the radio in the hut.

Since the enemy would frequently attempt (and, occasionally, succeed) to capture the Daytime Site, we could not remain overnight. Therefore, every night we would fly back to our Nighttime Site just as the sun was going down.

The Overnight Site, **_Lima 20 Alternate_**, or just **_Lima 20A_**, was in central Laos, closer to the PDJ (Initials for the Plaines des Jarres, or Plain of Jars, in Laos). Both sites were in enemy controlled country, and were guarded by local Muong tribesmen recruited by the CIA.

Lima 20A—the Overnight Site

This was a much larger place, with a real runway capable of handling fixed wing aircraft, and garrisoned with about 5,000 local soldiers. Unfortunately, the 'real' runway, dead-ended at the foot of a small karst (local term for mountain). This complicated take-offs and landings; sometimes forcing them to be performed with a tailwind.

A better view of Lima 20A – The Overnight Site.
Note the mountain at the end.

Most days were spent in utter boredom at Lima 36, our Daytime Site. There were several pilots who finished their entire year-long tour and never participated in a single rescue.

Speaking of tours, ours was a flat one-year. The fixed-wing pilots were allowed to rotate after 100 missions, but few Jolly pilots logged that many. Part of the reason was that we spent so much time on alert and part of the reason was in the way our missions were counted.

A fixed-wing pilot counted every takeoff and landing as a mission. We counted each trip 'North' (six takeoffs and landings), or a rescue, as a single mission. I was one of the few Jolly Green pilots to get a 100-mission patch.

When we did receive a call, we would scramble the two helicopters. One was designated "Low" (the pick-up bird), the other "High" (the back-up bird). We would alternate days as to which was "High" or "Low".

I am 'High' Bird on this Rescue

The general idea was that the 'High' bird would orbit somewhere nearby, while the 'Low' bird went in to attempt the rescue. If the 'Low' bird was shot down, the 'High' Bird was expected to immediately come and attempt to rescue everyone.

Sometimes, when this happened, the enemy was so busy celebrating the downing of the first helicopter that this technique actually worked. In theory, if both helicopters were shot down, everything would be put on hold until two more helicopters could arrive and begin the effort all over again.

Although we did _not_ succeed in rescuing everyone, it gave a great morale lift to the fixed-wing pilots to know we were there and would rescue them if humanly possible. Since I don't drink alcohol, I can't speak from personal experience, but it was said that no Jolly Green pilot had to pay for a drink at a fighter base during the war.

We were neither equipped for, nor allowed to attempt, night or foul weather rescues. Lacking night vision equipment, it was simply suicidal to fly into a heavily defended area with the lights on. Many an aircrew member was forced to spend the night or, worse yet, taken prisoner due to inclement weather and/or darkness.

All fixed-wing pilots were briefed to head southeast if they went down near the waters' edge or southwest if they went down further inland. Our sister Squadron at Da Nang (in Vietnam) handled the coastal and water pickups; we got everything else.

When we scrambled, both helicopters would fly in formation, homing on the emergency beacon from the distressed aircraft, or the PLB (Personal Locator Beacon) if the survivor had bailed out.

At the same time, a flight of four prop-driven, World War 2 vintage, A-1's, call sign "***Sandy***", would scramble out of Thailand and join up with the helicopters. Although the Sandy's were our primary support aircraft, Fast Movers (jets) could be called in when required.

The line of authority in a rescue mission was clearly established and never violated. En-route to the survivors' location, the lead Sandy was ***Mission Commander***.

What would happen was two of the Sandy's would streak ahead. It was their job to get a general fix on the survivors' position, positively identify him using authentication procedures, then troll for, and attempt to suppress, any ground fire that was encountered. The other two would remain with the helicopters until all were in the target area.

When the Lead Sandy felt the area was as secure as it was going to get, he would advise the Jolly Green pilot, who then took over as ***On-Scene Commander***. It was clearly understood, and never questioned, that the Jolly pilot had the final say, or right of refusal, as to whether the pickup proceeded. If he felt, for any reason, the situation was unsafe; he retained the right to scrub the mission.

After all, if he did proceed, he would be endangering not only himself and his crew, but another helicopter and four additional men who were in the backup bird. Although few Jolly pilots exercised this prerogative, it was there and understood by all.

Needless to say, performing a rescue was difficult, and often dangerous, work. A favorite trick of the North Vietnamese was to turn on a captured survival radio and tie it to a tree. Or, they would give the radio to an English speaker. In either case, they would set up some guns; then wait for the rescue helicopter to come along, and blow it out of the air. For this reason, pilots were briefed to destroy their survival radios if they were in danger of being captured.

Alternatively, the enemy could deliberately leave an American pilot alone, bringing in as many guns as possible, in hopes of shooting down the rescue aircraft when they arrived.

Helicopters, by their very nature, are extremely vulnerable to ground fire. A hit in the rotor blades has been known to unbalance and down a machine. (I knew of a helicopter that was downed by a single crossbow bolt. The shaft severed an oil line and the engine seized.)

The HH-3E had armor plating around the engines and both pilots sat in armored seats. There was a huge armored breastplate for each pilot that we were supposed to wear after strapping in. It restricted movement so badly I never wore it.

The Flight Mechanic and PJ would stack flak vests on the floorboards, hoping to deflect enemy bullets. Since the floorboards were also the fuel tanks, the aircraft was potentially vulnerable to fire caused by tracers penetrating the fuel tank.

Due to the noise generated by the helicopter, ground fire could not be heard. You could only "feel" the bullets striking the fuselage and see the tracers coming at you.

It was extremely difficult to spot a man on the ground. Often, due to the dense jungle, the survivor could not be acquired visually. I made some rescues by simply homing in on the man's smoke flare and lowering the hoist through the jungle, hoping that it was an American on the other end.

This is what it looked like, trying to find the survivor; watching and praying for smoke to drift up from trees that were 80 – 120 feet tall.

We carried our "Blood Chits", which made an offer of financial reward to anyone who would assist us. The "Blood Chit" is printed on silk and features a large American flag at the top, followed by a message in 14 languages (Burmese, Cambodian, Chinese, Chinese Modern, Dutch, English, French, Indonesian, Laotian, Malayan, Tagalog, Thai, Vietnamese, & Visayan), that reads:

"I am a citizen of the United States of America. I do not speak your language. Misfortune forces me to seek your assistance in obtaining food, shelter and protection. Please take me to someone who will provide for my safety and see that I am returned to my people. My government will reward you."

Blood Chit

In spite of this, someone in Washington came up with the bright idea of guaranteeing a reward and a free ride to a country of choice to any foreign national who materially assisted in returning a downed American airman.

Therefore, we were required to carry $10,000 in gold and various denominations to be paid on the spot. I don't know anyone who was very enthused about this idea, but we had to sign for, and carry, the money anyway.

The RCC (Rescue Crew Commander, or pilot) was responsible for it. We all had dark visions of some enemy pulling the pin on a grenade after he was aboard the helicopter; taking out everyone in a suicidal blaze of glory.

The top and sides of the helicopter were painted in jungle camouflage, while the bottom was light blue to represent a hazy sky. While this may sound silly, the second or so required to focus on the aircraft when it was flying over often meant the difference between taking rounds (bullets) or not.

Aerial view of jungle

HH-3E flying over the jungle

The above picture was taken about 20 seconds after the one on the previous page. Note how difficult it is to see the helicopter in the first picture. The camouflage paint *did* work.

Unfortunately, the HH-3E was unstable in flight. If the control stick were released, the nose would pitch up and the aircraft would roll inverted to the right in about 1-2 seconds. It was non-recoverable from this position. This was one more reason why we performed day pickups only.

We all had parachutes. In the event of fire or imminent crash, the RCC was expected to hold the aircraft straight and level until all the crew had bailed out. He could then attempt to bail out his window (there was not enough time for him to unstrap and walk to the back).

Since, as stated, the helicopter would pitch nose up and roll to the right, the RCC, who sat on the right, had little chance of getting out safely. He would most likely dive through the spinning rotor blades if he made it out the window.

Hopefully, the foregoing will give you a feel for the characteristics of the helicopter.

We wore a survival vest containing various items including, a survival radio, smoke flares and a shoulder holster with a .38 pistol. In addition, everyone had their own M-16, which was supposed to be kept in a locked gun cabinet until the need for it arose.

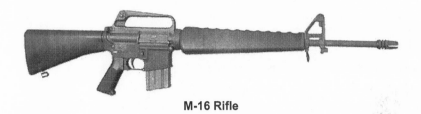

M-16 Rifle

Since I could not imagine what good a single clip of M-16 ammunition would do me if I were shot down, I illegally acquired and carried an AK-47 with a spare magazine. I kept it on the floor, right next to my seat. My thought was that there was lots of AK-47 ammunition among the ground troops.

AK-47 Assault Rifle

We did not fly as fixed crews, but on a rotating basis. I must confess that I was not the most popular RCC. I felt our job was to rescue the man _now_, not force someone else to do it later.

I would brief my crew when coming on alert of my concept of Air Rescue, which was that we were there to rescue people. My philosophy was that, once in a hover, we would stay until the survivor was on board. I also expected complete radio silence during the pickup unless someone was hit.

If either of the guys in the back were hit, I, or the co-pilot, would acknowledge the fact, but they could not expect much attention until we cleared the area. Everyone was to remain at their stations and concentrate on getting the survivor on board.

I informed the co-pilot that I would lock my shoulder harness on the way in, and expected him to do the same. If I were badly wounded or killed, I expected him to complete the rescue. The shoulder straps should hold me off the controls. If not, he could summon the PJ to roll me out of the way. The same would apply to him. Some crewmembers objected to my philosophy. When this happened, I would tell them to contact the Operations (scheduling) people and ask to be replaced. There were no hard feelings on my behalf.

During a pick-up, I would get as low as possible, actually nestling the belly of the helicopter in the trees. This reduced the amount of time it took the hoist to cycle up and down and, I felt, made me harder to spot then if I had been hovering at a higher altitude.

The run-in, or approach, was critical. The classic method was to fly straight in towards the survivor's position, gradually slowing down as you came closer, until establishing a hover over him. This tended to maximize our vulnerability, as it gave the enemy gunners a clear shot of a target with a steadily decreasing airspeed.

I came up with a (totally unauthorized) maneuver, which I felt minimized, my exposure. What I would do was to fly in towards the survivor at maximum airspeed until I was directly over him. I would then pull up into a near 90° vertical climb, roll the aircraft through 180° and drop the nose to the horizontal position. If performed correctly, in about 10 seconds I would go from around 120 knots to level flight at zero airspeed over the survivor, facing the opposite direction from before.

This maneuver was a little rough on the folks in the back, but I would warn them to hold on. It was also a little tricky to pull off, because the H-3 was absolutely non-recoverable from inverted flight. This meant I could not exceed 90° in any phase of the maneuver. I used this technique on nearly all my rescues. I have been told that this procedure was later briefed as standard procedure.

It was a 'big deal' when we rescued someone. There would be an impromptu party at home base when we returned with the survivor.

I dodge the water spray from a crew member who is being 'hosed down' after his first pickup

In the Officers Club we had a Jolly Green doll hung up in the bar with a placard carrying the rescue number on it.

My Co-Pilot and I change the number

"Meanwhile, back at the ranch," as they used to say, life at NKP was Spartan, but consisting of all the essentials.

The base included the usual amenities such as:

Armory   Where the weapons were stored. Before going on Alert, we would be issued our personal weapons from there.

Base Exchange/Commissary   Very small, with limited stocks of food and toiletries.

Control Tower   Even though I had an Air Traffic Control background from my enlisted days, I never visited the Control Tower.

Fire/Crash Rescue   Nice to know they were on duty, but I had no interaction with them.

Hobby Shop   There was both a Photo and Recording Hobby Shop. I took pictures on both slide and roll film with my bootleg camera and developed the pictures you see in this book at the Photo Hobby Shop. In the Recording section, there was a nice selection of recorded music. Since this was in the days prior to DVD's, CD's or even cassettes, I did all my recording on reel to reel tape. I used to play those tapes at home when I was stationed in Germany. Every 22 seconds there was an audible "beep", caused by the air defense radar as its antenna rotated.

Hospital   This is where the Flight Surgeon hung out. Fortunately, I had no need of his services.

Intelligence   The intelligence section was known as the TUOC (_Tactical Unit Operations Center_, the intelligence section where missions were briefed). Our last stop prior to assuming alert was there.

Life Support   Where our parachutes and survival equipment were stored and maintained.

Living Quarters   We were housed in long, wooden barracks called "Hooches". They were built up off the ground because the area flooded when it rained, which it did quite a lot. Each 'hooch' had a maid assigned, who did general cleanup and laundry. We all chipped in to cover her pay, but I do not remember how much it was.

Here I am in front of my Hooch

As I recall, there were about 4 bedrooms on each end, with a communal bathroom and showers in the center. Each room had 2 Officers assigned to it. We actually had 4 bunk beds, but normally only 2 men were assigned to a room.

I bought some bamboo curtains and my roommate and I screened off the beds from the front. Everything was a tight fit. For Christmas, my wife sent a small artificial tree which my roommate and I set up.

Christmas Tree – Note bamboo curtains in back.

The Front of Our Hooch

Mess Hall   Military mess halls have a poor reputation. Since Officers had to pay to eat there, I consumed all my meals in the O' Club.

Officers' Club   Or O' Club. Here, we could relax and order meals. The enlisted folks had their own clubs. I remember one day greeting the Thai waiter and asking for a hamburger. "No have hamburger," he replied. "No have hamburger?" I asked. "No, have cheeseburger, though," was his answer!

Personnel   There were personnel, or administrative offices, but I never visited there.

Police   An air base is essentially a miniature city. In the Air Force, the military police were called Air Police (often derisively called "Apes"), who performed the same function as police in a civilian town. Some years later, the Air Force changed their name to "Security Police".

Radio Station   There was a low-power, Armed Forces radio station, but I do not remember ever listening to it.

Runway   Obviously, there was a runway. Ours was made from PSP (pierced steel planking). Since I only used the first few feet of it, I do not remember its length. What I do remember, is that it unfortunately had a dip in the center, which partially filled with water after a rain. This puddle would extend across about 2/3^{rds} of its width and fixed wing aircraft had to be careful to keep to the dry side during takeoff and landing.

One day, an A-1 returned and accidently swerved into the puddle while landing. The plane slowly nosed over and ended upside down in the shallow water. The crash crews responded, but the whole thing happened in such slow motion, that they were in no particular hurry. Unfortunately, the pilot was stunned, the canopy cracked and the cockpit partially filled with water. When the crash crews arrived, the pilot had drowned.

Theater   There was a small theater which showed Hollywood movies. They would not start the movie until a certain number of patrons were in attendance. I can remember several times when my good friend and copilot would knock on my door and say we should go to the movie. If it wasn't a picture I was interested in, I would attempt to decline, but he would insist that we had to go anyway, because they couldn't start until more people showed up. So, I would go.

I love to eat popcorn during a movie. He would never buy any of his own—just steal mine during the show. Oh, the hardships of a combat assignment!

I am sure there were other departments such as civil engineering, etc. on the base, but I do not remember them.

The

Rescues

Returning from a Routine Mission - Jolly Green 1967

How embarrassing! Guess who got caught looking the wrong way as the picture was snapped? Here the guy is trying to thank me for saving his life and I am posing for the picture!

Over the River and
Through the Woods...

This rescue took place in November, 1967. Embarking on a 3 day alert trip up 'North', we took off early from NKP, planning to arrive at the Daytime Site (Lima 36) at first light.

As we were overflying the Nighttime Site (Lima 20A), however, my wingman announced he had hydraulic problems. He stated he thought it was just the gauge, and that the limited maintenance available on the ground should be able to repair it in a few minutes. I advised him I planned to continue on alone to Lima 36.

He reminded me that we were not authorized to fly single ship over enemy terrain, but I reasoned that he could catch up with me shortly, and as there was a heavy bombing schedule laid on for the day, I wanted to be close to the action in case we were needed.

Arriving at Lima 36 as dawn broke; I circled and buzzed the strip a few times. No one opened fire, so I figured that it still belonged to us.

I landed and we began to refuel from the fuel barrels. Not long after we had finished refueling and were assembled in the hut, we received a Mayday (emergency distress) call that an F-4 had been hit over Hanoi. We immediately scrambled and headed on an intercept course.

F-4

When the Sandy's caught up with me, they inquired where the other helicopter was. I told them not to worry; he would join us shortly.

As we 'homed in' on the aircraft's distress beacon, it became apparent that the pilot had headed WNW *toward* China, rather than SW away from China and toward Laos. This presented a problem. The United States was extremely worried at the time that the Chinese would find some excuse to intervene in Vietnam as they had in Korea. As a result, American aircraft were prohibited from flying near the Chinese border. Regardless, we continued to fly an intercept course toward the survivors.

As we arrived in the vicinity of the Black River (the northern and western limit of air operations), we realized we would have to cross the river if we were to rescue the two pilots. The riverbank was heavily defended, so we decided to climb to 10,000 feet and "jink" (maneuver from side to side) and spiral down as we crossed it. The flak (anti-aircraft fire) was heavy, but all five aircraft (one helicopter and four fighters) managed to cross without incident.

While we flew toward the area where the survivors were down, two of the Sandy's sped ahead to reconnoiter the scene, and the other two stayed behind to protect me.

Lead Sandy established voice contact with the pilot, who said he was about 2/3's of the way up a steep ridge, covered with razor grass. Because of the grass, he was not able to move. There was no contact with the back-seater.

As I entered the area, I spotted a steep ridge, which was clear of trees but covered with tall grass. At the foot of the ridge was a small hamlet. I observed several military trucks parked there. Some soldiers were busy setting up what looked like anti-aircraft guns, while others were attempting to cut a path up the ridge to the survivor.

Due to ROE (rules of engagement) restrictions, we were unable to open fire on them. I calculated we might have enough time to pick the pilot up before the ground troops reached him. At my instruction, the survivor popped his smoke. Now I knew exactly where he was on that ridge.

I began to ease the helicopter close to the ridge, hoping to be able to establish a hover over him. It was tricky work. There were strong crosscurrents of wind, which bucked the helicopter around. What complicated matters was the necessity to hover with my rotor tips just a few feet from the steeply angled ridge in order to get over him.

I went into my hover mode, which consisted of entrusting all aircraft gauges and radios except Guard (emergency radio frequency) to my co-pilot, and blocking out everything else as I concentrated on holding the helicopter absolutely still while the hoist was being lowered.

Out of the corner of my eyes, I could sense a brilliant, white light. What was that? Was the co-pilot shining a light in my eyes? That didn't make any sense, yet the light was there. Since I was busy maintaining the hover, I resolved to forget about it.

It was vitally important that the helicopter not be allowed to move even as much as a foot in any direction, or we would risk dragging the survivor through the sharp grass or, worse yet, knock the rotor blades off against the ridge.

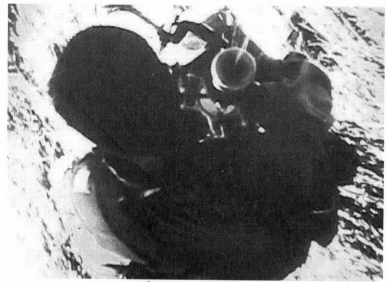

Survivor on hoist

Finally, the hoist reached the survivor and he began to climb onto the paddle seats. We had just begun lifting him off the ground when an enemy soldier rolled over the top of the ridge above me at a distance of about 75-100 feet. He aimed his AK-47 at us and began firing.

'Feeling' rather than hearing the bullets impacting the fuselage just below my seat, I yelled to the guys in the back that we were taking fire and transmitted the same message to the Sandy's.

In the meantime, the enemy soldiers' rounds (bullets) had continued to rise and tore into the rotor blades. The aircraft began to buck and jump as the blades lost their tracking stability.

At that time we flew our helicopters unarmed. Our only weapons were our personal M-16's. My PJ leaned out the door past the Flight Mechanic, who was busy operating the hoist, and emptied his clip into the enemy soldier. Without a doubt, he saved my life.

Our PJ was rather 'gung-ho', and had loaded his M-16 with straight tracer rounds. From the corner of my eyes, I saw a bright tongue of flame spurt from the cabin door and rip the head off the soldier, whose body tumbled down the ridge below me.

Due to the excessive vibration, I was barely able to hold the hover as we got the survivor on board. As soon as he was safely in the cabin, I pulled away from the ridge. The white light immediately snapped off.

The Sandy's, now freed of restrictions, were doing an enthusiastic job of obliterating the hamlet, along with the trucks and guns. The survivor called out that he thought his 'back-seater' was nearby, but we had more pressing problems on our hands.

A-1 rolling in to provide protective fire

The helicopter was vibrating. The vibration was so bad I seriously thought we might lose one of the blades. It was difficult to hold it steady as I turned toward home. Two of the Sandy's accompanied me while the other two remained behind to complete their destructive work.

As we were limping along, one of the Sandy's called out, "Don't look now, but it appears you have a MIG (Russian jet fighter plane) at 6 o'clock (directly behind) and closing!" They both went back to engage the jet while we pondered our next move.

Soviet made MIG fighter

The classic defense of a helicopter against a fixed-wing fighter is to head straight for your opponent and then autorotate (disengage the rotors and allow the helicopter to free fall). The high sink rate of autorotation, coupled with the jet's rapid closure speed should make him steepen his dive angle until he has to break it off. Then the helicopter can play tag among the ground clutter.

That is the textbook theory, at any rate. I had never heard of anyone actually trying it, and I wasn't about to be the first; not with the control problems we were encountering.

We could see the MIG as a faint speck in the sky. I slid over into a cloudbank, hoping he didn't have infrared missiles and would lose visual contact. We couldn't stay in the clouds for very long. I knew that the peaks of nearby mountains were poking up into those clouds and didn't want to smash into one of them.

The helicopter was still bucking and shaking. I didn't want to perform any violent maneuvers, as I wasn't sure it would hold together. When I couldn't stand it anymore, we dropped out of the cloud layer and anxiously scanned the sky.

My PJ shouted, "There! 10 o'clock!"

I pulled back into another cloud; still praying the MIG was guns only and didn't have infrared or radar homing on board. When we exited a few minutes later, we couldn't see the MIG anywhere.

Where had he gone?

"5 o'clock, high!" shouted my Flight Mechanic.

I plunged into a third cloud. This time, when we exited, the MIG was nowhere in sight. I can only assume he was low on fuel and had to head for home.

We plodded along our way, shaking and bucking, and were joined by the two Sandy's who had stayed behind to strafe the enemy.

Once again, we were approaching the Black River; this time from the North. There was no way I was going to attempt the 10,000 feet corkscrew maneuver we had done earlier. I was convinced the helicopter would fall apart if we tried.

Operating on my theory that "the closer to the ground I am, the harder I am to see and hit"; I flew at treetop level across the River while the Sandy's did their high altitude bit. The gunners were so busy trying to hit them we roared over in safety before they could realign the guns.

We began to notice a stiffening in the controls. Sure enough, a quick glance at the hydraulic gauge showed a fluctuating, decreasing pressure. We were losing hydraulic fluid! Some of that guy's bullets must have nicked a hydraulic line. This was a new and quite serious problem.

The HH-3E was a large helicopter. The flight controls were hydraulically assisted, much like power steering on a car. It was impossible for the flight crew to control the helicopter if hydraulic power failed completely.

I advised the Sandy's of our problem and that we might have to make an emergency landing. Looking around, I had no desire to set down in the vastness of the North Vietnamese jungle. I resolved to continue flying until the last possible moment.

After a while we heard the backup helicopter on the frequency. He had gotten his bird fixed and was looking for us. He met up with us, flew alongside and confirmed we had hydraulic fluid streaming out of the bottom of the aircraft.

My best estimate was that we were still about 30 minutes out of Lima 36. Our choice was to land there or crash into the rocks and jungle. There was simply no place else to go. At the same time, I was concerned about the 'back-seater' we had left behind. I hated to think an American was going to be lost when we had the ability to get him.

Finally, I directed the other helicopter to take the Sandy's and go back to try for the other guy. He protested that I would be left all alone, but I pointed out that if we didn't make the strip, our chances of survival in a crash landing were slim. After a bit, he agreed to make a try at rescuing the 'back-seater'.

Wonder of wonders, we made it to Lima 36. As I was attempting to set it down, I lost control and fell the last ten feet or so, resulting in a huge bounce and one of my worst landings to date. But, we were on the ground and safe. Praise God!

I shut down the engines amid cheers from the crew. As we started to kill electrical power, we heard the other helicopter transmitting a Mayday (emergency) call. A 57 mm shell had severed his tail rotor shaft. He wasn't sure how long he could maintain level flight and wanted help.

57 mm Gun

I was heartsick. We had just barely made it on the ground ourselves. Nevertheless, I was not about to abandon him. I told my crew I could fly the bird by myself. They should wait with our survivor until I got back. _If_ I got back. They were a good crew, and refused to remain behind.

I handed my M-16 to the survivor and told him to sit inside our wooden hut with the gun aimed at the door. He was to shoot anybody who tried to enter that didn't speak English. His eyes got very wide. I told him if we weren't back in an hour, we weren't coming back.

In that event, he was to wait until just before sunset before he dismantled and discarded the weapon. Then he should walk toward the fortress on the hill, with his hands in the air, shouting, "American, American". Perhaps they would take him in. A replacement alert crew was due in three days, after all, and they would get him out.

He didn't look too happy with the situation, but accepted the rifle. We got fired up and took off toward the other helicopter, which had a real problem. Unless they maintained 50 knots of forward airspeed, the helicopter would corkscrew, making any landing doubtful.

We pulled alongside them, shaking and vibrating quite badly. Sure enough, his tail rotor was completely stopped. Both helicopters turned and headed back, eventually getting Lima 36 in sight.

Now, we had a different sort of problem—whoever attempted to land first would most likely crash, thus denying the very short strip to the other helicopter.

I was certain I would not be able to make another safe landing, but there was a chance for my wingman. I told him to come in at 60 knots, plop it on the ground at the start of the strip, shut everything down and ride the brakes, hoping he could stop before going over the cliff at the end. He did a great job in getting his bird down in one piece.

Now it was my turn. As we came in for the landing, I lost control about 10-20 feet in the air. The helicopter hit hard. The left gear partially collapsed (apparently my first hard landing had weakened it) and the helicopter tilted over 45° on its left side, resting on the sponson.

In the process I wrenched my knee quite severely, but otherwise, everyone was OK. So there we were, towards noon on our first day of a three-day alert; one survivor, 8 crewmembers and two broken helicopters.

We took a look at the bullet damage. There were a few holes starting just below my seat on the right side. It was obvious the shells had come in my open window, passed in front of both pilots and exited through my co-pilots' open window. I felt as though God must have been working overtime, protecting me from harm.

I asked my co-pilot what the business was with the light shining on me during the pick-up. He got a funny look on his face and said he didn't know a thing about it. He hadn't noticed any light.

It was only later, when I encountered the light again during my second rescue and with a different co-pilot, that I began to believe it was the Shekinah glory of God, protecting me from harm. Every rescue I made, that light was there, disappearing when I pulled myself and my crew out of danger. I have no other explanation for it.

There were also holes in the rotor blades. That was the source of our vibration. We radioed in our status and were advised to standby—three helicopters were being dispatched. We felt like celebrating. We would get to go home early!

With the Survivor

A few hours later, three helicopters landed. The crews got out and they and the survivor climbed on the third bird.

"What about us?" we asked.

"You have two more days of alert to serve before you can come home," they replied.

That was my first rescue of the Vietnam War. In my official Mission Report, I omitted the details about my landing and then taking off again, as I felt that information might get me in trouble.

A few weeks later I was present when my helicopter, minus engines and rotors, and with the left gear firmly locked back in place, was sling lifted and flown to Bangkok for repairs. Several months after that, I flew to Bangkok to pick the helicopter up after it had been repaired.

There it goes! My helicopter departs for Bangkok

Another shot of my Helicopter leaving

I received the Distinguished Flying Cross for my actions that day.

THE UNITED STATES OF AMERICA

TO ALL WHO SHALL SEE THESE PRESENTS, GREETING:

THIS IS TO CERTIFY THAT
THE PRESIDENT OF THE UNITED STATES OF AMERICA
AUTHORIZED BY ACT OF CONGRESS JULY 2, 1926
HAS AWARDED

THE DISTINGUISHED FLYING CROSS

TO

CAPTAIN DAVID A. RICHARDSON

FOR
HEROISM
WHILE PARTICIPATING IN AERIAL FLIGHT
3 November 1967

GIVEN UNDER MY HAND IN THE CITY OF WASHINGTON
THIS   19th   DAY OF   January   19 69

Years later, landing at an Air Force Reserve Base in Florida, I noticed several HH-3E's parked there. One of the serial numbers looked familiar, so I walked over for a closer look. Sure enough, I could see the patches on the right side beneath the pilots' seat. It was the same helicopter I had flown on my first rescue mission.

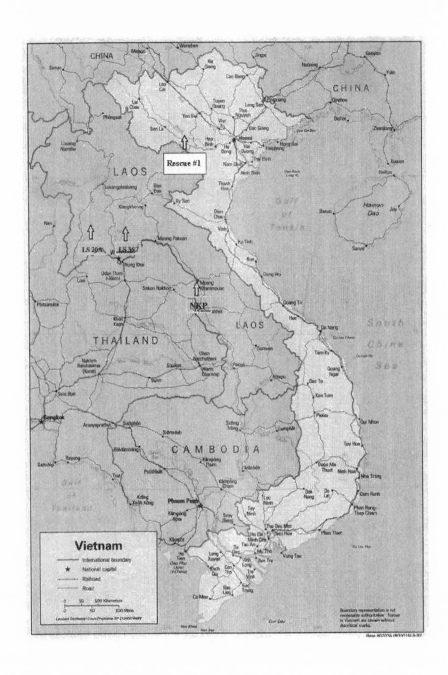

Stormy Weather...

My second rescue also took place in November, 1967. We were in the alert shack at Lima 36, when the Mayday call came in. An F-105 had been hit and was heading our way. We immediately launched, even though the weather was not good. The Sandy's joined with us and we proceeded toward the point where the survivor was down.

F-105

As usual, two of the Sandy's went ahead to check out the area, while the other two stayed with the helicopters. Soon, Sandy Lead called back to say he had arrived at the survivors' general area, but the weather was worsening and the cloud cover would probably be too dense to allow a pickup.

This, unfortunately, was an all too common occurrence. Many times the Sandy's, who would arrive in the area first, could find breaks in the overcast, which would cloud over before the helicopters arrived. In that case, the rescue would have to be called off. I had failed to rescue several pilots because of this.

Sandy Lead and I had been talking about this type of situation. The plan we had worked out was that if the Lead Sandy could find a large enough break in the clouds, he would descend through it and orbit near the survivors' position under the cloud layer.

Here is my friend, attempting to fly in formation with me

The idea was that when I arrived overhead, Sandy Lead would key his mike, holding the transmission open. Homing in on his signal, I would make a pass or two until I felt we were directly overhead. Then I would let the helicopter straight down though the clouds, trusting the Sandy pilot to keep sufficient clearance so that I would not descend into any mountain peaks. (And, incidentally, also hoping I would not ram the A-1 as we dropped out of the clouds!)

This was *not* an authorized maneuver. We had talked about it, but this would be our first try. Sandy Lead got in position under the clouds and, upon my command, keyed his mike while orbiting. Sure enough, when I arrived, I was above a solid overcast. When I got the needle swing indicating passage of his position, I initiated a zero forward speed vertical descent.

Talk about being nervous! We were letting down through solid clouds into a valley that was surrounded by jagged rocks. Our descent seemed to take an eternity, but was probably not more than a few minutes. We could see absolutely nothing out the windows, and I had to constantly adjust to keep us roughly centered above Sandy's orbit.

When we broke out through the cloud cover, there was just a few hundred feet clearance between the tops of the trees and the bottom of the clouds, with rocks all around. We had to maneuver some to get to the survivors' area. At my command, the survivor popped his smoke, which took us some time to locate as the wind wafted it around and up through the dense jungle growth.

When we felt we were overhead, we dropped the hook and prayed he was in the vicinity, as the smoke had blown and twisted and turned as it came up through the trees. I had the belly nestled down in the tops of the trees, as usual, making sure not to move even an inch as the jungle penetrator dropped to the ground.

There was that light again. This time I was ready and actually derived great comfort from it.

Finally, we had the survivor in the helicopter. The light went out. I applied power and began a shallow climb to get out of the area. During the time it took to make the pickup, the weather had worsened. Sandy Lead, of course, had climbed back up over the cloud layer and I was now stuck below, all by myself.

Pulling the Survivor into the helicopter

As I climbed, we were immediately in the clouds with absolutely no idea which direction to go! This was something I had not anticipated. The Sandy's, and my back-up helicopter, were overhead, above the cloud layer, so they could not help me.

The problem was that the peaks and rocks were buried in the clouds and neither the others nor I had any idea of the rocks' location relative to our position. We were trapped. Our only option was to continue. I did a maximum power, spiraling climb, up through the overcast, praying that we would not run into anything solid.

It was an agonizing time. Finally, after what seemed like hours, we broke through and were back on top of the cloud layer and able to set a course for home. God had spared me again.

Survivor exiting the helicopter

When I got back to NKP, Sandy Lead and I talked it over and agreed the plan needed some refinement before it could be recommended to others. But, as always, the important thing was that we had brought back the survivor.

I received another Distinguished Flying Cross (my 2nd) for my actions that day.

THE UNITED STATES OF AMERICA

TO ALL WHO SHALL SEE THESE PRESENTS, GREETING:

THIS IS TO CERTIFY THAT
THE PRESIDENT OF THE UNITED STATES OF AMERICA
AUTHORIZED BY ACT OF CONGRESS JULY 2, 1926
HAS AWARDED

THE DISTINGUISHED FLYING CROSS
(SECOND OAK LEAF CLUSTER)

TO

CAPTAIN DAVID A RICHARDSON

FOR
EXTRAORDINARY ACHIEVEMENT
WHILE PARTICIPATING IN AERIAL FLIGHT

18 November 1967

GIVEN UNDER MY HAND IN THE CITY OF WASHINGTON
THIS   21st   DAY OF   June   19 68

WILLIAM W. MOMYER, General, USAF
Commander, Seventh Air Force

Harold Brown
SECRETARY OF THE AIR FORCE

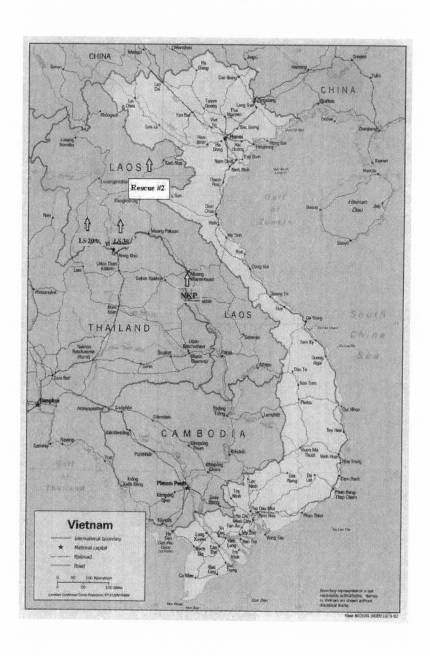

POSTSCRIPT

A similar situation presented itself at a later date in a different area. My friend, who was Sandy Lead once again, flew on ahead and encountered the same situation. He radioed back to ask if I was game to try it again.

I answered in the affirmative, and he announced he was starting to let down through a small break in the clouds. His next radio transmission stopped abruptly in mid-sentence. We never heard from him again.

After calling for several minutes, we scrubbed the mission and returned home. I decided that perhaps this method of Air Rescue was not the best. At any rate, this was the last time I attempted it.

Taken just after I landed at Lima 20A during a rainstorm.
A terrible picture, I agree, but it shows how bad the visibility got.

Ring of Fire...

My third rescue took place in March, 1968. It proved to be an unusual mission in that it originated from NKP, rather than our northern bases.

The Air Force would routinely conduct round the clock bombing raids on those portions of the **_Ho Chi Minh Trail_** that passed through Laos. To facilitate night bombing, a C-123 cargo plane (call sign **_Candlestick_**), would fly overhead, dropping high intensity flares which descended on tiny parachutes. They gave enough light to allow the fighters to see the targets.

C-123

One night, as this operation was underway, a C-123 was hit in the right wing. As a consequence, the right engine caught fire. After a few moments of bright glare, the pilot managed to put the fire out by activating the fire extinguisher bottle.

During the ensuing intercom check, the 'flare-kicker' failed to check in. When they sent someone to the rear of the aircraft to check, all they found was an intercom cord blowing in the wind. Evidently he had bailed out during the fire. They immediately called in a Mayday (emergency) and proceeded home.

Crown (call sign of the orbiting communications relay aircraft used in Vietnam), who was orbiting high overhead, established radio contact with the survivor, and told him "Keep your head down; Jolly will be in at first light to pick you up." We monitored the call and made what preparations we could, prior to turning in for the night.

The next morning, we briefed and departed so as to be in the area at first light. Upon arrival, we discovered the bad news. The road network in that area formed a rough triangle around a small karst, or mountain.

Our survivor was on the mountain, inside the triangle, which was about a mile to a mile and a half on each side. The road complex was, of course, heavily defended. Fast-movers (jet fighters) were brought in who attempted to neutralize the defenses, but it was a no-go. There were simply too many guns in the area for us to be able to knock all of them out.

Then we had an idea— if we massed our firepower and attacked just one spot in the line, we might be able to blow a hole big enough that I could slip through. We lined up everything we had and attacked the middle of one side of the triangle. I came in as fast as I could, right on the heels of the fighters, counting on them to be able to open a hole in the defenses big enough for me to get in.

It worked! We got inside and began heading for where we thought the survivor was hiding. We raised him on voice and spotted his smoke. I did my trademark maneuver. As I entered the hover, tracers from bullets were flying everywhere. My white light showed up during the hoist time and I welcomed it as an old friend.

We got the survivor on board, but had to do a lot of dodging and weaving as we headed back for our hole in the road's defenses. Imagine my consternation when I discovered the enemy had moved in mobile AAA (anti-aircraft artillery) during the pickup sequence!

We were now trapped inside the triangle and drawing heavy fire. I started zigzagging around the small mountain, trying to keep it between us and the worst of the guns, which was a joke, because there were guns on every side. The jets began attacking again, but they were having trouble clearing a path for us.

Finally, they told me to avoid 2 of the corners of the triangle (where the guns were the heaviest) and a particular side that they were going to try to open up. They massed everything again on the opposite side from the earlier attack and repeated their operation of blasting a hole large enough for me to get through.

I had a merry time trying to avoid being shot down as we dodged and turned on the slopes of the mountain, trying to use it to mask us from the worst of the ground fire.

Finally, they announced they were ready to make the attempt. As soon as I got the "Go!" signal, I flew up the side of the mountain, crested the top, and dove toward the area they had just bombed. It worked fine; God was with me. Once again, I had enough room to shoot across the road, this time to safety, just as the light blinked out.

Safe at last

I received another Distinguished Flying Cross (my 3rd) for my actions that day.

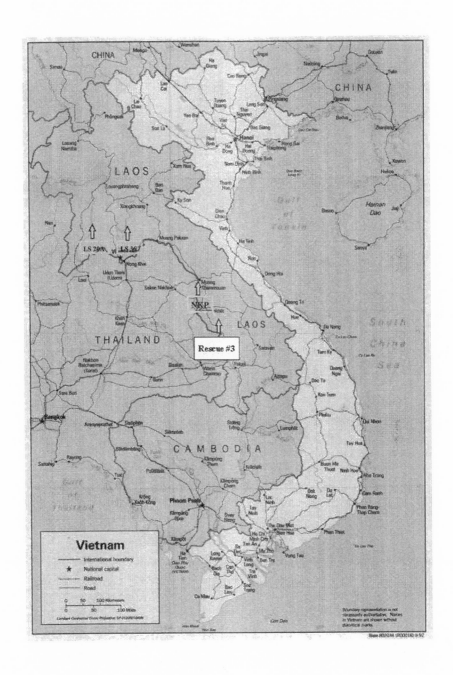

Refueling from a C-130

Approximately 2/3's of the way through my tour, our Squadron received a new Operations Officer, who managed, single-handedly, to take the Squadron morale from sky high to rock bottom. He had a SAC (bomber) background, and considered himself to be God's gift to wherever he was stationed.

He was particularly galled that, since he had low helicopter time, he had to fly as a co-pilot. He started implementing all sorts of needless "make work" policies that merely served to harass the Squadron members.

Unfortunately, our Squadron Commander was a weak person, who let the Operations Officer run rampant.

For reasons I will not go into here, the Operations Officer took an especial dislike to me. Perhaps it was because I stood up to him and some of his more worthless policies.

At any rate, he managed to make the last third of my tour miserable.

Interior of the Helicopter

Forgotten Mission...

This rescue took place in April, 1968. I was completely flabbergasted to find this pickup recorded on the back of my flak map. I had forgotten all about it.

I was instructed to fly single ship, as I recall, to a particular map co-ordinate and hoist whoever I found there into the helicopter, then fly to another designated point and lower him to the ground.

We arrived at the location and entered the hover. The white light flashed on. I was a bit apprehensive, as I did not know whether I was facing an enemy or not.

Finally, we spotted someone on the ground and began the task of hoisting him aboard. As we departed the area, the white light disappeared. The person I picked up was not an American.

When I returned, I was advised to forget what I had just done.

Why or how we were tasked to pick up a foreign national, I have no idea. I do remember that at one time, I got into trouble when I filed a very short mission report and I suspect it was this mission.

What I wrote was, "Sighted survivor, rescued same."

I did not receive any awards for my actions that day.

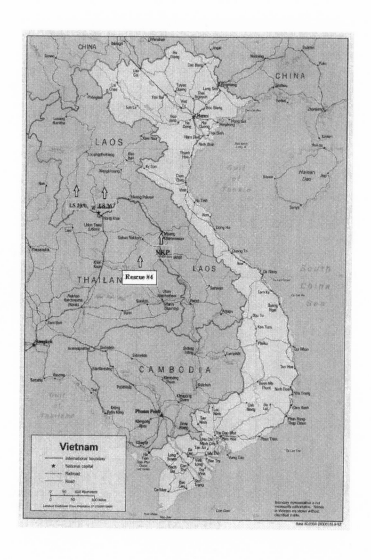

Schoolhouse Blues...

This rescue took place in May, 1968. When it came time to retrieve the repaired, battle-damaged helicopter from my first pickup, I was the logical person to fly to Bangkok and pick it up. The Operations Officer, however, vehemently opposed this, as he felt it would be a reward for me. I kept my head down and stayed out of the in-fighting. Finally, the Operations Officer was overruled and I was assigned the mission.

The idea was that we would put two full crews on one helicopter and fly to Bangkok. Then I would fly the repaired bird home while the other crew would return in the helicopter we flew down in. Due to the flight time involved, and the general nature of things, we would stay at least one night in Bangkok. For this reason, there was considerable competition in the squadron to be on the second crew.

When the big day arrived, I demanded that I be assigned to fly the helicopter to Bangkok. The Operations Officer showed up at our briefing, in a very surly and threatening mood. He demanded that I take-off on time, fly straight to Bangkok, spend only one night there and return directly to NKP. No deviations would be allowed. If I failed in any of these considerations, he would 'roast me alive' when I returned.

It was with almost childish glee that I took off some 20 minutes late. We had had a maintenance glitch; nothing that could be blamed on me, but I was inwardly smirking.

We flew on a nearly direct line toward Bangkok, paralleling first the Laotian and then the Cambodian border. Some time into the flight, we picked up a distress call from an Army Special Forces group near the Cambodian border.

They had wounded in critical condition and were requesting immediate evacuation. We listened with interest. This wasn't our concern. The Army had its own helicopters for Medevac; ours were strictly for the rescue of downed aircrew and we were not even on alert.

After awhile, it became obvious that the Army was not going to be able to send any help. The requests became more desperate. There was a fear one or more of the wounded might die. Unwilling to allow fellow Americans to die, I radioed in and offered our services, which were immediately and gratefully accepted.

The others aboard cautioned me that we were not authorized to perform this mission, but I was not going to abandon my countrymen just because of some technical details. We were vectored in by radio. It turned out that, due to the heavy jungle, the only place we could land was in the yard of a small school.

I made a pass overhead. The spot was rather small, but it looked as if we could fit in. Basically, it was a small yard, surrounded on three sides by tall jungle. On the fourth side were three buildings in a line. The end buildings were single story while the center building was two stories high. The small outbuildings were separated from the main building by driveways.

I landed in the schoolyard and taxied up close to the cluster of buildings. The kids had all been let out of school, naturally, and were standing around watching. I swung the helicopter around so that my tail was toward the buildings. They brought three men out on stretchers and loaded them inside the helicopter.

Wounded being loaded

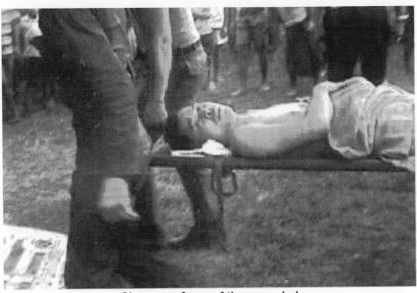

Close-up of one of the wounded

As we prepared to leave, about ten additional Special Forces troops jumped on board. I tried to pick the helicopter up into a hover, but we were overloaded.

The School and Special Forces

I told my Flight Mechanic to order those who were not wounded to get off, as I could not lift the helicopter off the ground. They refused to do so; claiming that their position had been overrun and they would most likely be killed if we did not take them. There was no way was I going to leave Americans behind under those circumstances, so I let them remain on board.

It _is_ possible to get an overloaded helicopter off the ground by doing a running take-off, similar to a fixed-wing aircraft. As the helicopter gains speed, it will acquire "translational lift" and can be coaxed into the air.

Taking a long look at the schoolyard, which appeared to be about three times the length of my helicopter and barely wider than my rotors, I decided, after a moment's hesitation, that we might be able to do a running start and get airborne, even though the wind would not be in our favor.

So, I began taxiing toward the far end, hugging the tree line on my right as close as possible so we would have room to turn around. The ground was rough and full of potholes, so we were forced to taxi very slowly.

When we were about halfway down the field, I saw a man step out of the jungle on my right and point an AK-47 at me. There was absolutely nothing I could do. I thought for sure I had 'bought the farm', as the saying goes.

After sighting directly at me, he turned to his right and began firing at about a 45° angle in front of me. I yelled to the others in the back and the Flight Mechanic fired at him with the door gun, which practically tore him in half. (I mentioned earlier that I had a low opinion of the usefulness of the guns. This made me a believer!)

I could not understand the man's strange actions, but had little time to worry about it as I was approaching the end of the field and wanted to get out of there.

It was only after I returned to home base and recounted my adventures, that I understood what had happened. One of the other pilots remarked that the troops were trained to aim directly as an aircraft and then swivel and fire; 'leading' the plane much as a duck hunter would 'lead' a flock of ducks in flight. Apparently, no one had thought to tell this guy that there was no need to 'lead' an aircraft that was taxiing on the ground!

When we got to the far end, I turned around, pulled in full power, held the stick forward, and began rolling as fast as I could directly toward the school buildings. At this point, I had several problems. One was that there was a quartering tailwind; the second was that it was difficult to gain any real speed as we bounced along through the numerous holes; and the third was that I had to be able to clear the buildings at the end.

As we lumbered along, trying to coax enough ground speed to get translational lift, the children, who were lined up along the buildings were waving to us. As we neared the halfway point of the field, I realized we weren't going to make it. I also wasn't sure I could get the helicopter stopped without dinging a rotor blade, so I started pumping the cyclic (control) stick back and forth, desperately hoping to get airborne.

My friend, the white light appeared. Even though it hindered my vision, I welcomed it, as I felt I knew the source behind it.

The helicopter began hopping up and down as we roared toward the buildings, but was unable to maintain flight. The children stopped waving and scattered to each side. I had the sickening feeling we were going to crash straight into the school, but it was now too late to do anything but continue onwards.

I gave the stick a mighty yank and we were airborne! Unfortunately, we were only a few feet off the ground and gaining altitude so slowly I knew we would never clear the buildings. I lowered the nose, hoping to gain some badly needed airspeed, and aimed for the space on the left between the main and outlying building.

When we were within approximately 20 feet of the buildings, I gave another mighty heave on the stick. The helicopter jumped up and then began to settle. I immediately leveled the aircraft, trying to maintain altitude and gain airspeed.

We flew past the buildings with the fuselage between the buildings and our rotor tip path just barely above the roofline. The crew and passengers immediately broke into cheers. My co-pilot told me later that he had been sure we were going to crash and die.

The white light disappeared.

We slowly gained altitude and headed for the nearest Army hospital base, where we dropped off our grateful passengers and continued on our way to Bangkok.

Once there, we stayed overnight and prepared for a morning take-off. Unfortunately, my previously damaged helicopter that had been repaired had some problems, so the other crew left without us. I wasn't able to leave until the following day.

We had an uneventful flight back to NKP. Our arrival, however, was _not_ uneventful. The Operations Officer met the aircraft, breathing fire and brimstone.

He was threatening to Court-Martial me for disobeying all his orders. In addition, he was going to nail me for an unauthorized landing, an unauthorized rescue, and for "recklessly endangering aircraft and personnel", by picking up the Special Forces wounded. My defense was that I had saved 13 Americans, three of whom were so badly wounded they would most likely have died.

This, apparently, was not a good enough excuse. I was put on, more or less, confinement to quarters while my fate was pondered. I realized that I was in a very vulnerable position and that my career could well be over. As the days went by, the threats were reduced from Court Martial, to Article 15, to Letter of Reprimand, to Verbal Reprimand.

What helped was that the Special Forces sent a glowing thank you to the unit. Finally, as far as official action goes, the whole thing was just forgotten.

Friends urged me to press for 13 rescued, but I felt I should only count the three who were badly wounded. The others were mere passengers. The Squadron, however, refused to recognize _any_ of the people I had picked up as official rescues, so, in the end, nothing got counted.

I heard rumors that the Army had offered a Bronze Star or some sort of medal, but that it was rejected by the powers that be. I do not know if that is true or not.

Needless to say, I did not receive any awards for my actions that day.

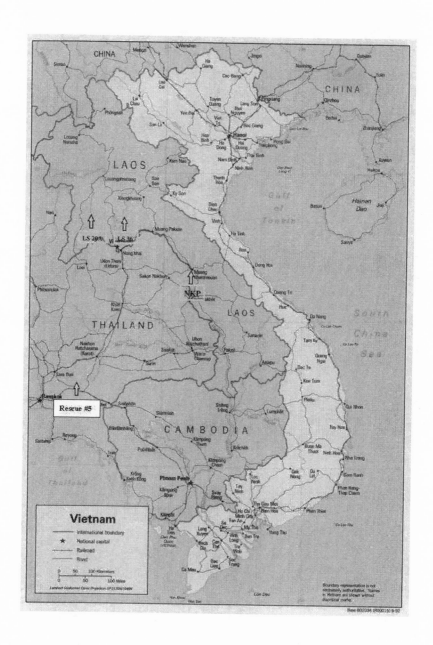

On the hoist

Rescues 6 & 7

These next two rescues occurred over a period of three days during which I attempted to recover a Navy pilot.

Before it was all over, 189 sorties had been flown with the loss of seven fixed-wing aircraft and one helicopter—all to rescue that one Navy pilot.

I will point out two items that might be of interest:

➢ In addition to the 5 aircraft specifically mentioned as lost in my narrative, there were several 'fast movers' (jets) that were damaged during the bombing effort and an additional 2 that were lost returning to their home base. I am not certain of their fate—whether they were picked up by the Jolly squadron at Da Nang or not.

➢ While this was my last rescue mission in Vietnam, it was the first mission flown by the survivor, so we had the irony of a first and last mission overlapping.

At the time it took place, this was the largest rescue effort of the Vietnam War and generated considerable public attention.

The pilot of the Navy A-7 that was shot down has written a superb book, "***The Rescue of Streetcar 304***", which does an excellent job of relating the rescue from the viewpoint of the man on the ground, waiting to be rescued. I encourage everyone to read it.

THE RESCUE OF STREETCAR 304

A NAVY PILOT'S FORTY HOURS ON THE RUN IN LAOS

KENNY WAYNE FIELDS

Yes, there are minor errors in the book; just as there are in any written work. I will give two examples:

1   I was _not_ sitting around drinking beer the afternoon of Day Two after rescuing the Sandy Pilot as stated in the book.

1st, I do not drink beer or any hard liquor.

2nd, I was flying orbits just outside the valley where he was trapped, waiting for the opportunity to rescue him.

3rd (if you need a third reason), it is against Air Force regulations to consume alcoholic beverages while on flight duty.

2   While he may have been fearful of
falling back out the cargo door after
being rescued; there was never any
danger of sliding across the cabin and
out the far side as described. Unlike
the UH-1, the HH-3E does not have
doors on both sides of the fuselage.

But these are minor quibbles. If you want to
experience first-hand what it felt like to be a downed
American pilot trying to stay alive behind enemy lines until
rescue arrived, this is the book for you. He will have you
worn out from vicarious emotions before the climatic ending.

A-1's in flight

I was nearing the end of my one-year tour as an HH3-E, RCC (Rescue Crew Commander) in Vietnam and had been taken off the duty schedule (as was the custom) for the few days left before rotating back to the States.

On the Tuesday before this event, I was asked if I would fill in with a final tour of alert duty at NKP since the unit, for one reason or other, was short of RCC's. The deal was that I would not deploy 'North' (to the Lima sites), where the action was, but merely stand-in as a back up at home base. Being somewhat bored, I readily agreed. The alert period would last from sunset Friday, to sunset Sunday. I won the toss for 'Low' bird for Saturday.

That was how I found myself picking up my equipment and crew, attending an intelligence briefing at the TUOC (Tactical Unit Operations Center, the intelligence section where missions were briefed.), and heading to the alert building on Friday afternoon. As usual, I timed our arrival to get there about 15 minutes early, so that the outgoing crew, who had been locked up for three days, could get on their way as soon as possible.

Just as we arrived, but prior to assuming the alert, a Mayday call came that a Navy A-7 from the carrier America had been shot down over Laos. The pilot had ejected and landed in an unoccupied valley. It was estimated that there might be just enough time to pick him up before darkness set in. The crew coming off alert immediately scrambled, while my crew and I watched them leave.

Navy A-7

After what seemed a long time, the rescue choppers returned, without the survivor. There _were_ people in the valley and the enemy resistance had been too strong to chance a rescue before darkness settled in.

The two Sandy's, who had performed the initial check of the area, had both run into trouble—one shot down (the pilot presumed dead due to loss of radio contact in spite of his wingman's sighting of a good chute), and the second, crashing while attempting a landing at NKP (which we witnessed). It was a sobering moment. It looked as though this rescue would be a difficult one.

That night, a delegation arrived at the alert hut from Operations with an offer to replace me. It was noted that I was not 'legally' supposed to be on alert and therefore was given the opportunity to back out of what promised to be a sticky mission. It was a tempting offer, but I did not feel I could live with myself if I backed out and my replacement was injured or killed, which seemed likely, so I declined.

We were up at about 0300 for the mission brief at the TUOC (Tactical Unit Operations Center, the intelligence section where missions were briefed.). The news had not changed. Intelligence confirmed there were numerous enemy troops and equipment in the survivor's last known area. We launched in time to be in position at first light.

The weather was terrible; heavy cloud cover over the area. Our two helicopters orbited a short distance away while the fast movers (jets) attempted to suppress the enemy's defenses.

We continued our orbiting until our fuel gages indicated 'Bingo' fuel (minimum amount necessary to return to home field). I advised Control that both helicopters were returning to home base. This was overruled, as it was felt that an attempt for the rescue was imminent.

So, instead of us flying back, a C-130 tanker was called in. Flying out to its orbit area, I plugged in and filled our tanks.

Just as I dropped off the tanker and my wingman was hooked up, we were advised that they thought the guns had been silenced enough to attempt the rescue. Was I willing to give it a try? I said we might as well take a look.

Newspaper Publicity Photo – Taken after Rescue #7

120

A Ridge Far Enough...

As usual, two fighters were sent in at low level to locate and identify the survivor and check for ground fire. The lead fighter was immediately blasted out of the sky.

We received a Mayday (emergency) call that one of the Sandy's, had been hit and was going down. Fortunately for him, he was able to zoom his aircraft up before ejecting and his chute carried him across the ridge on the far side and out of the valley.

Control immediately cancelled the attempt for the Navy pilot, but wanted to know if I could get to the Sandy pilot.

I told them we would give it a try and headed in.

A-1H Skyraider "Sandy" escort aircraft

I managed to do an end run around the valley and get to his position before the enemy knew what was happening. Since we were unable to raise him on the radio, we were forced to locate him by homing in on his radio beacon. I dropped my external tanks and went into a hover.

I could feel God's presence as my old friend, the white light, showed up. As I hovered over the spot where the survivor was on the ground, we could see him clearly, lying among trees which were approximately 75 feet tall. He wasn't moving. At first I feared he was dead or severely injured. I hesitated to put my PJ down, as this always complicated matters.

Finally we saw him stirring about, so I had my Flight Mechanic drop the rescue hoist in front of him. He noticed it and climbed onto the paddles, allowing us to bring him up through the trees. We encountered only light enemy fire.

No awards were given for this rescue.

With the Survivor

Back on the ground at NKP

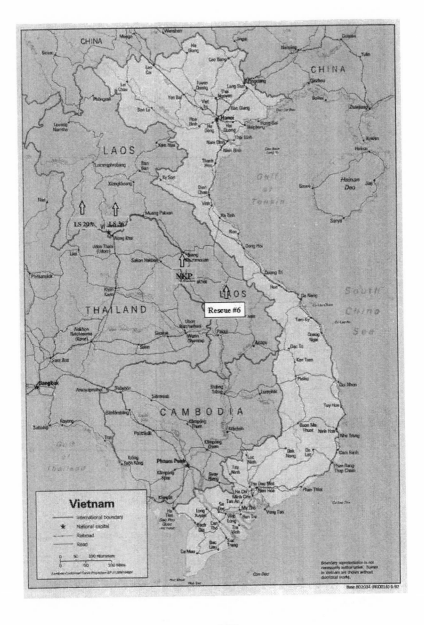

Since the weather had socked in, both helicopters were cleared to RTB (return to base) with the survivor. My co-pilot and I had lunch at the O' Club while the two birds were refueled and mine was re-equipped with new drop tanks.

During lunch I was again approached with the offer to be replaced. My feelings about the matter had not changed, so my answer was the same as the night before. My co-pilot, however, announced that he felt one rescue a day was quite enough and asked to be relieved. A new co-pilot was assigned, and we once again took off for the staging area.

Not too long after arriving at our orbit point, we were alerted to the possibility of a quick pick-up attempt, only to be told it was a false alarm. I continued to orbit for the rest of the day; orbiting just one ridge away from the survivor. So near, yet so far. It was very frustrating, but there was absolutely no chance of making the pick-up due to the weather and, especially, the guns.

As nightfall approached, our spirits lifted. Unable to perform night rescues, we knew we would be allowed to RTB (return to base) very soon.

The onset of darkness and 'Bingo' fuel were both fast approaching. I had just told the crew we would make one more orbit before requesting permission to depart, when a message came crackling over the radio:

"Jolly 16"

"Go."

"Jolly 16, you are ordered to perform the rescue immediately."

"Say again," I asked.

The message was repeated. "Jolly 16, you are ordered to perform the rescue immediately."

"By whose orders?" I replied. "I am the On-Scene Commander. It is my decision and I am not ready to make the pickup."

Back came the answer.

"The Commanding General of 7th Air Force in Saigon personally orders you to make the rescue immediately, regardless of cost."

Oh boy. I had a sinking feeling in the pit of my stomach. It was obvious we would not be able to survive such an attempt at this time. Considering the amount of personnel and guns in that valley, to hover in darkness (which was fast approaching and would be on us by the time we got to the survivors' position) was tantamount to suicide.

I mentioned earlier my confidence that God was assuring me I would return, and that regardless of the circumstances, I could always feel the hand of God on me. That was _not_ true in this case. I felt as though God's mantle of protection had slipped from my shoulders. I knew that if I entered the valley that evening, I would die.

But, orders were orders. Several A-1's were quickly formed up which proceeded to lead me up a gully or ravine which led down from the crest of the ridge. The idea now, since I was low on fuel and darkness was imminent, was that rather than flying to the mouth of the valley and backtracking, as planned, we instead would pop over the ridge and dive down to where we thought the survivor was located.

As we headed up the ridge, the ground fire was severe. Operating once again on my theory that a low-flying helicopter is harder to see and/or hit than a high flying one, I dropped to about 20 feet above the bottom of the gully and followed the Sandy's.

The guns on the surface were not able to depress their gun barrels enough to hit me. The Sandy's were flying above, shooting at anything that moved. Gradually, however, due to the slower speed of my helicopter, I began to fall behind.

As we were twisting and turning, clawing our way toward the top of the ridge, I lost sight of the last Sandy. It was then I clearly saw some men throw a camouflage tarp off a gun position in the bottom of the gully a few hundred yards ahead of me. They began firing as they traversed the gun toward our helicopter.

I banked hard right, thinking to fly up over the side of the gully, which was about 30-50 feet high, to avoid flying directly over the gun, but there was heavy fire pouring down on us. I then rolled to the left, only to find the same situation. By this time we were nearly over the gun position. I called for help from the fighters, held the helicopter in a right bank and ordered my Flight Mechanic to "***Take out that gun!***"

He emptied an entire belt of M-60 ammunition into the position, silencing the gun. (Once again, the gun I had spurned saved my life.)

The Sandy's returned, blasting the guns on the edges of the slope, and led me to the top of the ridge, where my relief was short lived. I could clearly see the muzzle flashes of the guns in the valley, which was in near darkness.

I can only describe the sight by comparing it to a Fourth of July celebration I had once attended. As the patrons entered the amphitheatre, each was given a candle and a match. When the darkness was complete, the people struck their match and lit the candle. The myriad flashes were soon displaced by a steady, blossoming glow from the candles. That was what the ground fire in the valley looked like as I began my dive into it. I thought, "We're dead." And then, "Lord, why did it have to end like this?"

Just then a radio message blared, "Jolly, abort the mission. Abort the mission and RTB (return to base)".

I didn't need to be told twice. I reversed course and headed for the safety of NKP. When I arrived back at home base, I angrily demanded to know just what had happened.

The answer went something like this: It seems the Navy, noting that this was the second day of the rescue effort, had sent a message to the Air Force asking for a progress report on 'their boy'.

As it happened, the Commanding General was out; so his aide, acting on his own authority, sent the "rescue at all costs" message out, over the General's name. When the General returned, he immediately countermanded the order.

I was assured that the policy was intact; the Jolly pilot, as ***On-Scene Commander***, retained the final go/no-go decision. This didn't matter much to me at this point, as I would be the high or back-up bird in the morning.

Back at the alert hut, I huddled with my crew. It was my feeling that if anyone had to make the pick-up, it should be us. We were the only ones who had had a peek into the valley and I felt we would have a better chance than someone who was totally unfamiliar with the terrain.

The crew was extremely dubious until I pointed out that if the "Low" bird was shot down (as seemed likely), we would have to go in anyway, to rescue them along with the original survivor and then we most likely be shot down as well.

Since we had had a look at the valley, I felt I could get us in and out safely, if we were rescuing just one person; certainly not five. They agreed, so I sent my co-pilot to the Operations folks with the suggestion—which was firmly refused.

That night (Saturday), a general meeting was held to discuss our strategy and the prospects of rescuing the survivor. Things did not look hopeful. So far, every aircraft that had entered the valley at low-level had either been shot down or badly damaged by ground fire. There seemed to be no way to enter the valley and accomplish the rescue without sacrificing one, or several, helicopter crews.

We discussed asking the survivor to attempt to move to a more favorable area, but this was vetoed on the grounds he had already moved a significant distance; was beginning his third day and therefore doubtlessly exhausted; and, most importantly, the presence of so many enemy forces increased the chance of his capture.

It was evident to all that the chances were high that the enemy knew his location and was leaving him as bait, hoping to shoot down a few more aircraft.

Then someone mentioned a type of gas, which could render a subject unconscious for 20 to 30 minutes. It was thought that a few A-1's from the Vietnam coast, call sign "*__Spad__*" could be converted with spray bars overnight.

The plan began to take shape. A heavy bombing would take place, followed immediately by the gas aircraft, then, right on their heels, the helicopter, which would find a large enough spot to land, when, presumably, all of the enemy would be unconscious.

This would give the crew, wearing gas masks, about 20 minutes (they hoped) to wander around in the jungle trying to find a now unconscious survivor. I thought the plan was one of the dumbest things I had ever heard; but being a mere Captain, when I voiced my opinion, I was ignored by the Colonels in charge (who would not have to attempt this idiotic maneuver).

We were advised to get some sleep and be ready to lift off at "oh-dark-thirty" once again. Later that night, my roommate sought me out and said he had heard I had volunteered for this mission.

When I said, "Yes", he said he had also heard that it was going to be a particularly rough mission the next day. When I allowed that this was apparently the case, he bet me a nickel I wouldn't come back alive.

I took off just before dawn, with a new helicopter. Since it was almost universally agreed we would most likely lose the first and probably the second bird, we took 3 helicopters instead of the customary two. (That gave me a wonderful feeling!) On the way in, I practiced flying with a gas mask on.

Me, flying with Gas Mask on

We reached our orbit area (a different one from the previous day, nearer the mouth of the valley) and settled in.

Word came that they were having trouble outfitting the gas tanks on the A-1's and we should be patient, so we continued our orbit for what seemed like several hours.

The survivor advised us he had moved to a new area during the night. He was now in a large clearing with trees about 80 feet tall around him. He stated that the ground was covered with tall razor grass and that there was a pile of rocks near the center where he was hiding.

The only glitch was that the enemy was climbing those trees and hauling heavy machine guns to the tops, with the barrels pointed inward. He felt they knew where he was and were only waiting to blast the helicopter to shreds as it came to a hover.

That made the gunners in the treetops an obvious hitch to our plans. The gas cloud would be, at most, 20 feet deep, so there was little chance the gunners in the trees would be affected by it.

To counter this problem, it was decided to use CBU's (_Cluster Bomb Unit_; a bomb filled with steel ball bearings), fused to explode at treetop height to knock them out.

Suddenly, my radio crackled. The low Jolly was experiencing hydraulic fluctuations and beginning to have control difficulties.

I immediately advised him I was assuming Low bird status and he was cleared to RTB (return to base). I ordered the third helicopter to fly cover for him in case he went down. Suddenly, in the blink of an eye, my status changed from backup bird to the primary pickup helicopter with no back up.

Home base advised they were scrambling an additional two helicopters to our area to act as our back up, but it would take at least an hour for them to arrive.

I later learned that the damaged helicopter was forced to make an emergency landing short of our home base and that the number three bird picked everyone up successfully.

The next thing I knew, we heard the survivor calling, "I'm hit, I'm dying; please help me!" Or, words to that effect. One of the CBU bombs failed to detonate at altitude, exploding instead on top of the survivor, shredding his legs and torso.

I thought, "Oh boy, this really rips it!" I switched to another channel to check on the gas birds. They were at least an hour away from launch—the same story we had been hearing all morning. The backup helicopters from home base said they were now at least 45 minutes out.

What to do? Rescue procedures dictated a back up helicopter in place before attempting a rescue. If the Low bird was shot down, the back-up helicopter was the Low bird crews' only chance.

Yours truly

Into the Valley of Death...

There was a sudden lull in the radio transmissions. I realized everyone was waiting for me, the **_On-Scene Commander_**, to make up my mind.

There really wasn't much choice:

First   Air Force policy did not allow a rescue attempt without a backup helicopter.

Second   the ground fire was too heavy.

Third   the gas birds, which would eliminate the danger of ground fire would not be ready for another hour.

Fourth   it seemed unlikely the survivor would live long enough for us to pull everything together.

Fifth   the only rational decision was to send everybody home before we lost more aircrew and aircraft.

Realizing all this, I transmitted, "Jolly is going for the pickup".

Someone replied, "You don't have to go, Jolly".

I replied, "Jolly 09 is going for the pickup, get me some fighter escort".

I believe it was six A-1's that formed up to lead me in.

There was, naturally, a high degree of anxiety among my crew. The site was not adequately prepared, and there was no back up if we ran into trouble. In addition, I strongly suspected a trap; that we would be shot out of the sky as I came into my hover.

We had to pickle (release) our drop tanks sooner or later. So, in an attempt to calm the crew, I authorized my co-pilot to drop the tanks at will and bet him and the crew a steak dinner for each that he could not hit a small sandbar in the river directly ahead of us.

This focused the crew's attention on something other our predicament. Wouldn't you know--he hit the sandbar squarely with both tanks? This caused some laughter as I grumbled I now was out three steak dinners.

Then, suddenly, we were in the valley. Operating on my usual "the closer to the ground I am, the harder I am to see and hit", I flew at treetop level as we fought our way up the valley toward the survivor. The sky was a swirling mass of fighters. Tracers were flying, and rockets were screaming. Further and further into the valley we flew.

A-1 rolls in to protect me

I was extremely worried as we fought our way down the valley. Since the day I had arrived in-theater, I had heard stories of how the enemy would use a captured radio and an English-speaker to lure the helicopter into a trap. This was the third day of the rescue attempt and so far we had been unwilling to risk allowing a helicopter to enter the valley.

Now, suddenly, the survivor was claiming to be badly wounded. It didn't sound to me like the same voice I had heard Friday evening, all day Saturday and even earlier that morning. I felt almost certain that I was being suckered. I knew I had the authority to terminate the mission and no one would blame me. And yet—what if there really _was_ an American, badly wounded and desperately waiting for me to rescue him? I had to go on, but I was filled with apprehension.

The clearing the survivor had described came into sight. I told him to pop smoke, but there was no answer and couldn't see any smoke.

Again, I requested smoke. Still, no answer. I couldn't see any smoke and, due to the thick ground cover, I couldn't see the survivor.

The scene appeared to be one of total confusion as the fighters continued to weave about us, firing everything they had. I was still concerned. There was no survivor in sight. _Was_ this whole thing a trap? As I slowly moved into the clearing, I radioed, "If you don't show yourself in ten seconds, we're outta here".

Then I realized how foolish this must seem to a badly wounded man who probably couldn't pull himself out of the brush. Questions, questions, questions. _Was_ this a trap? Should I put my PJ down?

Then my Flight Mechanic called smoke off to our right, and I drifted that way and went into my hover mode, which consisted of blocking out everything else as I concentrated on holding the helicopter absolutely still while the hoist was being lowered.

We could still see his smoke, but it was blowing parallel to the ground and we couldn't see the survivor. I knew if I moved the helicopter even as much as a foot, the hoist could tangle in the dense undergrowth. Still unable to visually acquire the survivor, I hovered and waited for him to come to us.

My comforter, the brilliant while light, was there again, brighter than it had ever been before. I waited. And waited and waited. People all around were shooting at us. Was the survivor already dead from his wounds?

This was foolish. If I continued to hover, I was going to get myself and my crew killed. Reasoning that I had promised him 10 seconds, I decided to wait a just bit longer and began counting to myself before taking us out of there to safety. Finally, the survivor was spotted. We got him on the hoist and on board. I pulled in full power and began moving up and forward. The light blinked out.

I was jinking madly to avoid the guns, which were still firing on us. As we cleared the area, the PJ yelled to fly straight and level, the survivor had passed out and he was attempting to stop his bleeding before he died.

No way was I going to fly back down that valley. I headed straight toward the same ridge I had crested the night before, straining to gain enough altitude to clear it. As we neared the top of the ridge, a gun I had not noticed above us, began firing as its crew attempted to depress their muzzle sufficiently to hit us. I rolled sharply to the right, but had to immediately reverse as we almost collided with an A-1 just off to our side.

As I rolled level, he fired two rockets, which blew the gun position away. We were so close we both flew through the debris cloud. Once again, the PJ was yelling to fly straight and level as he thought the survivor was dying and he was trying to operate.

We got safely over the ridge and headed for home. It was then that I realized we did not have enough fuel to make it back to NKP. I had allowed my co-pilot to punch off the drops too early.

So—we had to request a link-up with a refueling C-130. I was suddenly getting a lot of practice in aerial refueling!

Me, refueling from C-130 tanker

The survivor told me later that the crew awakened him so he could watch a helicopter refuel. We got our tanks filled and were able to resume our journey to home base.

As usual, when we arrived back at home base, a gigantic crowd of well wishers was waiting for us.

Me with part of the crowd after we got back

We got the chopper shut down and the survivor taken care of. In the midst of all the festivities, my roommate came up and said, "I see you made it back."

"Yup," I replied.

"Here's your nickel," he said, and presented me with a nickel (which I still have today) for winning the bet.

As the crowd was backslapping and congratulating us, a pilot came forward and asked who the Jolly pilot was. I told him it was me. He shook my hand and said he was the pilot who had fired the rockets into the gun position and saved both our lives.

The Survivor being carried to an ambulance

He also said that was all he had left; he was out of bombs and 20mm ammunition and those were his last two rockets. I shook _his_ hand. If he hadn't been such a good shot we would both have been dead.

Then he showed me his aircraft, which resembled a piece of Swiss cheese. He said he had never gotten below 150 knots and yet his plane was riddled with bullet holes!

He also said he had punched his instrument panel clock when I went into the hover and again when I moved out. The clock showed I was absolutely stationary for over **_four minutes_** while everyone was shooting at me. He wanted to see my helicopter.

We walked around my bird. There wasn't a single hole in it! He thought I had switched aircraft and was playing a joke on him and left in anger. I silently thanked God for once again keeping both myself and the crew safe.

141

The Sandy pilot had said I was in the hover for four minutes; it seemed more like 10 minutes to me. If you want to get a tiny feel for what those four minutes were like, try this exercise: Four minutes is 240 seconds. Sit down in a chair and, holding all parts of your body perfectly still while staring at the floor, begin slowly counting (one thousand, one; one thousand, two, one thousand, three, etc.) from one to 240 while imagining people on all sides are shooting at you. Four minutes is a _long_ time.

Here is a side story that may be of interest: After this mission, and just before leaving for home, I received a letter from my wife. Everyone who has met my wife, Kaye, agrees that she is a Godly woman. In the letter, she said that one night, she was awakened from sleep by our young son who said 'they' were trying to hurt his Dad.

Filled with a deep sense of urgency that I was in danger and in much need of prayer, she immediately got on her knees beside her bed and began earnestly praying for my safety. After a few minutes, she felt a calmness descend on her and returned to bed.

The following morning, she wrote me the letter I was reading, describing the incident, noting the time and date and asking if I had been in danger. Naturally, she knew nothing at that time of this mission.

When I received the letter, I compared dates and, adjusting her time to the time zone where I was, discovered that she had been prompted to pray for me at the exact time I was in the hover! God does use His children in mysterious ways.

The following night (Monday), after my safe return to base, my co-pilot and I visited the survivor in the base clinic. Shortly after that, I rotated back to the States on schedule.

Here we are, with some of the Sandy pilots after the Pick-up

Before I left, a story circulated around the squadron that the Navy had asked for the names of the crew who performed the pickup, supposedly to put us in for the Navy Cross, but that the Operations Officer, whom I had had problems with, sent them a roster of the entire squadron, saying it was a team effort. I do not know if this was true or not.

I received the Silver Star for my actions that day.

THE UNITED STATES OF AMERICA

TO ALL WHO SHALL SEE THESE PRESENTS, GREETING:

THIS IS TO CERTIFY THAT
THE PRESIDENT OF THE UNITED STATES OF AMERICA
AUTHORIZED BY ACT OF CONGRESS JULY 9, 1918
HAS AWARDED

THE SILVER STAR

TO

CAPTAIN DAVID A. MCFARRSON

FOR

GALLANTRY IN ACTION

1 June 1968 to 2 June 1968

GIVEN UNDER MY HAND IN THE CITY OF WASHINGTON
THIS 25th DAY OF NOVEMBER 1968

I thought about this particular rescue many times, but had no contact with any of the participants. 30 years later, the phone rang one day and when I answered it a disembodied voice asked if I was Jolly 09, the pilot that had rescued Streetcar 304 in June, 1968. It was one of the Sandy pilots from that mission. He told me they had been looking for me—the Air Force had asked those participants who were still alive to come to Nellis AFB in Nevada to brief the **_Air Force Fighter Weapons School_** on rescue techniques. He wondered, would I like to join them?

It was there that the survivor and I met once again, 30 years after the events of those fateful days. I also met the Sandy pilot who was shot down on the first day. All this time I had thought he was dead, but it turned out he had been captured and spent 5 years as a POW.

After the affair was over, he came up to me, said it was good I had gotten 'Streetcar' out and asked why I had not picked him up since he was barely a mile away? I told him there was no radio contact; we thought he was dead.

He paused a moment, then said he saw me, I practically flew over him on the way in for the pickup, why hadn't I just swerved and collected him? I told him again, we thought he was dead and that I certainly would have gotten him also if we had known he was there.

He paused again, then nodded his head and said he knew it wasn't my fault, but "5 years as a POW was hard". Then he turned and walked away.

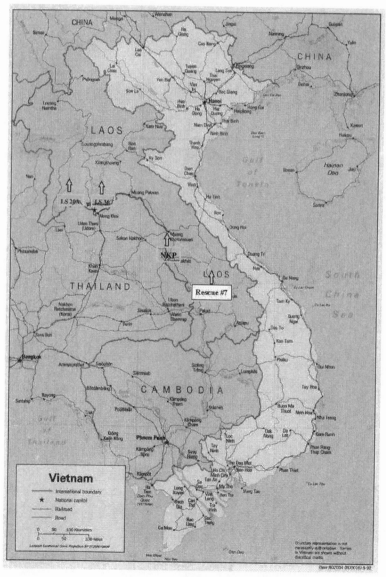

Newspaper Publicity Photo – Taken after Rescue #7

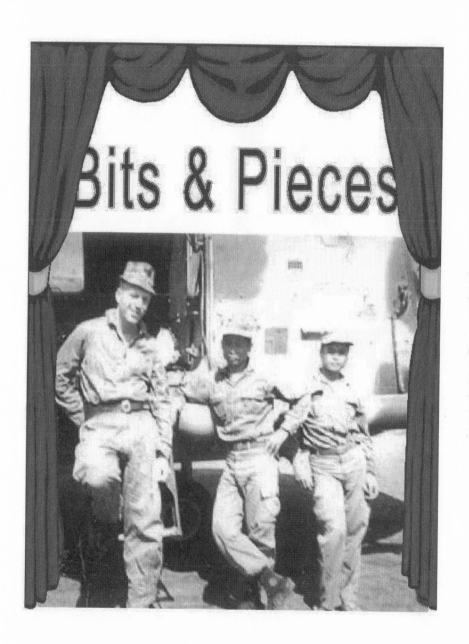

Before We Got Our Guns

Bits 'n' Pieces

During the year I spent in Southeast Asia, several things happened to me that were not strictly part of a rescue story. In this section, I will attempt to relate a few non-rescue experiences. They are arranged in alphabetical order.

Me at Lima 36, inspecting a 'spider hole' defensive position

_AK-47_   Apparently my quest for an AK-47 became common knowledge. One day, while I was eating lunch by myself in the O' Club at NKP, a guy I didn't know asked if he could sit down at my table.

We struck up a conversation, and he finally casually mentioned he had heard I was looking for an AK-47. When I admitted that was true, he asked what I intended to do with one.

I told him my thoughts about substituting it for my M-16 in case I got shot down. He allowed that that was a good idea, made some small talk, and left.

About a week later, he showed up again and asked me to join him outside. When we were alone, he gave me a wrapped package, advising me not to open it until I was in a private spot. I didn't see him again, but I was pretty sure he was CIA (Central Intelligence Agency).

Back in my room, I opened it and there was an AK-47 with two loaded banana clips. Even though it was against regulations, I kept the AK in a locker in my room and carried it on all my missions from that point on. Fortunately, I never had to use it.

CAMERAS   Because of the fiction that there were no Americans operating in Laos, we were expressly forbidden to carry cameras or take pictures when flying up 'North'. I made it a habit to smuggle my 35mm camera along and took several shots which I developed myself at the base photo hobby shop. That, for the most part, is where the pictures in this book came from. It is true that the pictures reproduced here are of varying quality; just keep in mind that some of them were taken under trying circumstances, when precise adjustment of the camera was not possible, and that all were scanned over 30 years after the event.

CHARIOT ON FIRE   I believe this incident took place to the south, southwest of Hanoi. I remember that the ground fire was extremely heavy, with the Sandy's buzzing all around us. Suddenly, I heard a tremendous explosion and we started losing power.

Unable to maintain a hover, I began to pull away. Looking up over my left shoulder and slightly behind me, I could see a hole about the size of a large grapefruit in the cabin roof. There had been some ZSU 23-4 guns in the area, but from the size of the hole, it is more likely that a 57mm gun hit us.

We had lost the right engine. Fuel was pouring out of severed lines and sparking electrical wires had set it on fire. Following established procedure, I gave the order to bail out, and everyone moved to the aft ramp. Trailing smoke and flames, I struggled for altitude so the others could bail out. They waited for me to get high enough that their chutes would open.

We were still attracting a fair amount of ground fire, especially from a small ridge directly in front of us. Attempting to escape the tracers, I rolled sharply right and pulled the nose up. The change in our angle of attack blew the flames out.

I was ecstatic. As we continued our single engine climb, I told the crew what had happened, and that I felt I could fly the helicopter all the way back to NKP. They were free to accompany me if they desired.

None of them were too keen on bailing out over enemy territory, so they elected to stay with me. I told them I would maintain a high enough altitude on the flight home that they could bail out if it became necessary. Just then, the fire re-ignited, but I was able to once again put it out by banking hard to the right and pulling the nose up. So we flew all the way back alone, periodically blowing the fire out.

As we crossed the border into Thailand, I declared an emergency, reporting that we had had a fire. Just before landing, I did my maneuver, putting the fire out. Then we dropped it on the runway and immediately shut down everything before it could start up again.

There were all kinds of fire vehicles around us. They looked rather disappointed that we weren't "crispy critters". The top of the helicopter was blackened, but it did not catch on fire again. I could not take a picture of the helicopter because we weren't supposed to carry cameras and there were too many people around.

People were crowded around, congratulating us, when my nemesis, the Operations Officer, came up and ordered me to report to him in his office. When I showed up, he threatened to Court-Martial me, saying Air Force Regulations required a crew to bail out when their aircraft is on fire.

I pointed out that I had brought back an aircraft, which could be repaired, and four lives (counting myself). I also pointed out that I would certainly have died and the others would have been captured as POW's, had I attempted to follow those regulations. He began raving about my insubordination and how he was finally going to get me for this latest transgression.

I said, "Do what you have to do, Colonel" and left. Although I had a few anxious days, I never did hear anything more about it.

CLOSE CALL   We had to fly a circuitous route across Laos to get to our sites. Although there was a TACAN (aerial navigation) station not too far from our daytime site simply called, North Station, it was of little use to us at our low altitude.

As a result, one had to make several trips with an experienced pilot, memorizing rocks and trees, before he could be checked out as an in-country RCC.

On one particular flight, I was training a newly arrived RCC candidate on the route to our sites. The weather was bad, as usual, and we were flying beneath the low-lying cloud layer.

Normally we flew with the cockpit windows open, due to the heat and humidity, but this time I had the right window closed so I could keep the windblast off my map as the other pilot flew from the left seat.

The helicopter was bouncing about in the turbulence, and I dropped the pencil I was using to keep track of our position on the map. Somewhat aggravated, I strained to reach the cockpit floor, which was difficult to do with a bulky survival vest on.

I finally regained my pencil and straightened up to find a bullet hole in my side window at the level of my head. Apparently, the bullet went through my window, past the other pilot, and out his open window. If I hadn't dropped my pencil, I would be dead. Dropping my pencil saved my life. Sometimes on such small things hangs the thread of our existence.

COOKING FUEL   The native wives were responsible for keeping the cooking fire going. Matches were a treasured rarity in those parts; most of the fire starting was done with flint and steel or by rubbing two sticks together.

I felt sorry for these hard-working women, and managed to let them know I would give them some jet fuel whenever I was there. They would come down in a solemn group, with their tin cups or wooden bowls.

Wives of the tribesmen guarding Lima 36.
Note the dirty look I got for taking their picture!

I would slide under the helicopter and, using a stick, depress one of the check valves on the underside of the fuselage while holding their container in place. The jet fuel would burn very hot and helped to keep their water-soaked firewood going.

CURSE YOU, RED BARON!　　　One day, as we were sitting in our hut at the daytime strip, we heard the noise of an aircraft quite close, followed by the sounds of machine gun fire and explosions. Running outside, we saw an incredible sight: two enormous bi-planes were attacking the strip!

Soviet AN-2 "Colt"

As they banked around for a second pass, we could hear the deep chug of the .50 caliber gun emplacement on the hill opening up. We ran for our helicopters as they came in for another pass. Strangely, they were not shooting at us, but, rather, at the strip and the fortress on the hill.

Our helicopters seemed to be unscathed, so I climbed into the seat and began the start sequence. As I was getting the blades in motion, I saw another CIA (Central Intelligence Agency) helicopter fly up alongside one of the bi-planes. Someone in the cargo compartment of the CIA copter fired into the cockpit of the second bi-plane, which pitched nose down and went straight into the ground. The helicopter then began to chase the lead bi-plane.

Apparently, the pilots of the lead bi-plane were more concerned with the helicopter chasing them than with maintaining control, because they crashed head-on into a karst (local name for a mountain) and just slid down to the valley floor.

Since the show was over, I shut down my engines. The CIA helicopter landed and scrounged up some cable before flying over to the wreck of the lead bi-plane.

Although it took some time, they managed to jury-rig the cable around the wrecked plane and sling load it onto our dirt strip. Then they flew off, presumably to fetch reinforcements.

Wrecked AN-2

Realizing (correctly, as it turned out), that I might not have much time; I went over and inspected the downed plane. Although single-engine, it was enormous. The Russian designation was AN-2 and it was code-named "Colt" by the Americans.

The AN-2 was fairly large, with metal-covered wings and fuselage and fabric covered control surfaces. They were used to haul supplies around North Vietnam and were a fairly common sight.

Locals and me at wreck

This one was painted a dark olive green and had no markings on it. The three dead crewmembers had been loaded into the CIA helicopter before it left. I caught a glimpse of them and they were _not_ Asians.

I entered the fuselage through the large cargo hatch on the left side. Inside the cabin, the floor panels had been removed and rows of tubes installed vertically. These tubes had held mortar shells, secured in place by small trap doors which had a wire release attached to each one.

This, evidently, was their 'bomb bay'.
Also in the floor were Russian-designed oxygen bottles.

The cockpit was a mess. The single engine had been mounted just forward of the two-man cockpit. When the plane smashed into the rock face, the engine had collapsed back into the cockpit, killing both pilots.

The instrument panel was tilted and bent at a crazy angle. There were some maps in the cockpit, which showed a meandering route starting from the vicinity of Hanoi. I walked around the outside and discovered that there was a large rocket pod mounted under the lower wing on each side. Apparently their jury-rigged armament consisted of the forward firing rockets, the mortar shells dropped from the belly as bombs, and a man firing an AK-47 out of the cargo door.

Front view, note rocket pod under wing

Close-op of under-wing Rocket Pod

Hearing approaching rotor sounds, I was standing 'innocently' around when three CIA helicopters landed and disgorged several men. As they began examining the wrecked plane, one of them came over to me and inquired whether anyone had been inside the plane. I replied, truthfully, that no one else had been in the area and added that I was guarding it for them. He thanked me, and said I was free to go.

CUSTOMS   Central to the natives' faith as I understood it, was the belief that this world was a corrupt, evil place and that heaven waited only for those who obeyed the many rules in existence.

Since the head was the most distant from the ground (therefore, the closest to heaven), it was deemed holy. The rest of the body was graded in terms of increasing filthiness as one approached the feet. For this reason, one never touched the head of another. (Your hands are lower on the body than your head.) Quite a ritual was necessary to make the head 'clean' again if this happened. Americans, who love to pat children on the head, got themselves into real trouble this way. It was said that, early on, more than one American was banned from trips 'North' because of this.

Another problem was the American habit of crossing one's legs when sitting. Although seemingly innocent, it exposes the sole of one's foot to the other person. This was a deadly insult to them, the equivalent of saying they were lower than the dust under our feet.

Additionally, shaking hands was taboo. Once again, the hand is at a lower position than other parts of the body. Instead, one would fold his hands; bow the head and say, "Sa Wat Dee". These were only a few of the many other subtle mannerisms.

<u>*FLYING WITH THE CIA*</u>   I had another CIA (Central Intelligence Agency) contact while I was in SEA (Southeast Asia). I do not recall how or when we met, but he would somehow keep track of my whereabouts and arrange to drop in occasionally at our daytime site when I was there. He flew a <u>*Pilatus Porter*</u>, the propjet, single-engine STOL plane.

Pilatus Porter

Part of his job was to run, or check on, the many sites the CIA had in Laos—each manned by local mercenary tribesmen.

When the weather was bad and the bombing raids had been called off, I would occasionally fly around Laos with him. This was strictly illegal and I suppose I could have received a Court-Martial for it, but no one ever said a word.

It was fun and I got to see a lot of Laos and the shadowy, 'spook' side of the conflict that the others never did. We would drop in at some very remote sites and check on the progress of the war.

One day, we stopped at a small strip that, according to my friend, hadn't been visited for a few weeks. He had heard that they had been engaged in a battle and wanted to check the results. As we shut the engines down, we could hear a horrible commotion, screaming and shouting, coming from one of the huts. Grabbing our weapons, we ran to the largest hut, from which the noise was coming.

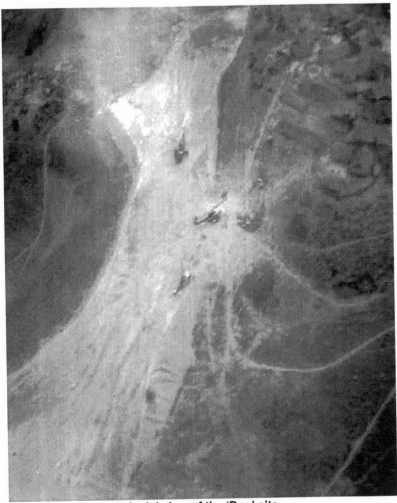

Aerial view of the 'Dog' site

I was dumbstruck at the sight that greeted my eyes when we entered. Four men were holding down another, wounded, man on a crude, wooden table. A sixth man was chopping or hacking at the wounded man's left arm with what turned out to be a rusty, dull, machete. The injured man was thrashing about, screaming, while the others shouted at him.

As we watched, the man wielding the machete missed, and lopped off the injured mans' ear. It was a mess; blood was everywhere. Finally, they managed to hack the wounded mans' arm off. The severed arm dropped to the floor, ignored by the men who were now trying to stop the massive flow of blood.

As I ran for a first aid kit from the plane, a stray dog rushed inside, picked up the arm and ran off. The rest of the men abandoned the injured man and began chasing the dog, trying to recover the arm. We finally got things calmed down and put a dressing on the injured mans' shoulder. As far as I know they never did get the arm back from the dog.

The injured man had been shot in the arm and the wound, without proper treatment, became infected with gangrene. The choice had been simple; amputate the arm or let him die. We had walked in during the "operation".

As terrible as it sounds that was the way things were done in this primitive place. Later I heard that the man died anyway, presumably from the shock of his 'treatment'.

FORTRESS   What we called a 'fortress' was mainly a conglomeration of small shacks made of wood and the remains of our fuel barrels. It was located at the top of a small rise near the end of our strip. Although 'off-limits' to Americans, I visited there once to observe the gun emplacements and homes.

**Lima 36 - The 'Fortress' at the left middle.
Our parking area is at right center.**

Fortress on the hill, built out of used fuel drums

View from the Fortress

LEOPARD SKIN COAT There were leopards roaming about in the jungle and I became intrigued with the idea of hunting them and having a leopard-skin coat made for my wife.

Obviously, I was in no position to hunt the animals myself, so I put the word out to the locals that I was willing to pay for each leopard skin brought to me. Within a few weeks, I had the five skins I deemed to be the minimum I would need. My next problem was to get them and me to Bangkok and to find a furrier who could transform the skins into a coat.

165

I was able to get myself on a trip to Bangkok where I found a furrier who was willing to do the job. I specified that I wanted all the scraps of unused fur saved and returned to me with the coat. A few weeks later, I again went to Bangkok and picked up the coat and the fur remnants. In true "White Hunter" style, I sewed a strip of leopard skin around the base of my Derby hat and put out a notice that I would provide the fur to any other pilots who had made a rescue. Overnight, this became both a fad and a source of recognition for those who had performed a pick-up.

Eventually, I mailed the coat to my wife, who gallantly wore it on several occasions. It turned out the curing of the hides was not done properly—the resulting coat weighed a ton.

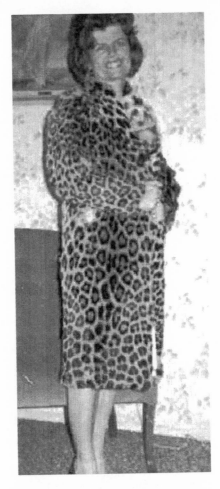

LETTERS HOME   When I first arrived at Udorn, I had to report in to the Squadron Commander, who asked about my parents and family. When I told him both my parents were alive and that I was married with a wife and 2 children, ages 6 and 4, he told me I was to spend the rest of the day writing 5 letters.

He said that, as an RCC (Rescue Crew Commander), I would be responsible for the lives of 3 other men (my crew) as well as a valuable helicopter, and that the survivor on the ground would be depending on me.

He pointed out that I would be asked to enter an area where a jet going 500 miles per hour had just been shot down; and that my airspeed would be about 100 miles per hour. I would be required to hover completely still for several minutes, perhaps while under fire, to get the survivor on board.

As the On Scene Commander, I would have the responsibility of determining if risking my life and the lives of my crew for just one man was worth it, especially considering that if I got myself shot down, a second helicopter and crew would feel obliged to attempt to rescue me.

He said he felt he should also mention that my chances of being killed during the year I was there were quite good and wanted to know if I felt up to all this. When I answered in the affirmative, he told me I was to write a letter to each of my parents, thanking them for their love and support as I was growing up and including anything else I wanted to say as my last words to them.

He added that, statistically, after I died, my wife would marry another pilot within a year and that someone else would raise my children, who were too young to remember me. Therefore, he wanted me to write a letter to my wife, expressing my love and regret that death had separated us and granting her the freedom to continue on with her and the children's lives in whatever way seemed best to her.

I was also to write an individual letter to each of my children, telling them anything I thought they should know about their Dad and how sorry I was that I wouldn't be there to help them grow up.

Then, I was to seal the envelopes and return them to him. He would keep them in his safe and only mail them after I had died. In the event I survived, the letters would be returned to me, unopened, when I left for home.

LOST MONEY   I have already mentioned the $10,000 in gold and various currencies we were required to carry as a payoff to locals who assisted an American pilot to escape.

My roommate had the misfortune to lose his packet on a trip 'North'. He signed for the packet, as usual, when he left the TUOC (Tactical Unit Operations Center), but when he arrived at his aircraft the gun locker (where the money packet was stored) was locked and the Flight Mechanic, who had the key, wasn't around.

Not wanting to carry the money around with him, he shoved the packet between the gun locker and the side of the fuselage, intending to place it inside later. Unfortunately, for him, he forgot about it until he returned to NKP after three days and six flights. Naturally, it was missing, and no one would admit to having seen it, so he had to report it as lost.

The Operations Officer, whom I had problems with, did not care for my roommate either. (Sometimes I think this was only because of my roommate's association with me.) So he decided to press the issue and hold my roommate responsible.

In fact, he called for a formal investigation and named me as the _Squadron Investigating Officer_. Since my roommate was a good friend of mine, this appeared to me to be a clear case of conflict of interest. I went to the Operations Officer, protested my appointment, and asked to be relieved. He refused to replace me, insisting he wanted my roommate prosecuted to the full extent of military law. I was really up a creek. I think the Operations Officer took special glee in making me the person to ruin the guy.

Before I assumed my new responsibilities, I asked my roommate why he didn't just say the packet had been lost during enemy action over North Vietnam instead of admitting he did not know what happened to it. He said that he hadn't thought of that in time.

What to do? Once I had my appointment in writing, I could no longer talk freely to my roommate since I was now his opponent in a legal sense. In fact, I could not discuss my investigation with anyone even after my report was submitted.

The Operations Officer began bugging me to get this obvious open and shut case closed as soon as possible. I got a copy of the UCMJ (Uniform Code of Military Justice) in an attempt to see what had to be done. The Operations Officer had already told me he would _not_ accept a recommendation for either a _Letter of Reprimand_ or an _Article 15_ (One of the lesser forms of Court Martial in the military); he wanted my roommate before a full Court-Martial if at all possible.

As I read over the Regulations, it became clear that what we were talking about was negligence, which was covered thoroughly. I was determined to somehow get my friend off with the least possible fine or sentence. But I also had to consider my own position. If I fumbled or fudged this assignment, I could be liable for charges myself.

There seemed to be no way around the charge of negligence. What my roommate had done was rather indefensible. After all, he _had_ left the money packet lying around unsecured. There seemed to be no point in speculating who took the money. There were seven other crewmembers between the two crews who had both access and opportunity to discover the packet.

Obviously, the members of my roommate's crew were the prime suspects. Of them the Flight Mechanic was the most likely, since he had the key to the gun locker and would have been rummaging around near it. But, any of them could have found the packet and no one would own up to even knowing it was there.

I was heartsick as I read the follow-on charges, which could be levied against my friend if he were convicted under the negligence section. I discovered, there are two types of negligence: _Simple_ and _Gross_. I was determined to get the guy off as easily as I could, so at first, I leaned toward simple negligence. It sounded so innocent and common. After all, gross implied a terrible event or transgression, while simple sounded so, well, simple.

As I read on, however, I discovered an interesting caveat. The charge of gross negligence was the harsher accusation and much more difficult to prove, but, since it was such a harsh accusation, a person convicted of gross negligence could not be punished further.

Simple negligence, on the other hand, could (and usually did) lead to further charges and much stiffer punishment, including fines and possible imprisonment.

An idea began to form in my mind. If I could aggressively press a charge of _gross_ negligence and get it to stick, my roommate would suffer little more than embarrassment while being exempt from further prosecution. I realized this would be a tricky stunt to pull off. I was certain the Operations Officer would never allow me to do what I was planning if he were totally aware of the consequences. He wanted the guy to fry.

So, I reported back to the Operations Officer that negligence seemed to be the appropriate UCMJ charge and that I favored gross negligence rather than simple. Naturally, I did not inform him of the end results. He was ecstatic. I am sure he thought I was caving in to him.

The next two to three weeks were some of the hardest of my life. To prove gross, rather than simple, negligence, I had to aggressively go after both my roommate and the witnesses I called. As the days went on and I pressed harder to get people who were sympathetic to my friend to support my harsher claims, everyone, including my roommate, stopped talking to me. They were all certain that I had sold out to the Operations Officer and was trying to curry favor. My roommate even went so far as to request that he be assigned to another room, so he could get away from me, but this request was refused, making my job even more difficult.

Finally, the investigation was over and I submitted my report recommending gross negligence. The Operations Officer enthusiastically signed and forwarded the finding and my friend became guilty of gross, rather than simple, negligence.

Once the report was received and accepted by higher headquarters, my new buddy, the Operations Officer, as I had expected he would, told me to start preparing general Court-Martial charges based on the gross negligence finding.

He was enraged when I informed him that the matter was closed, and no further action could be taken after a finding of gross negligence. When word got out to the Squadron, there was general amusement and several officers apologized to me for their remarks and actions toward me during the investigation. We never did find out who took the money.

MAIL   Mail from the States was abysmally slow, often taking up to three weeks. My wife and I wrote each other every day but, due to the lag time, often would go for a week or more without receiving anything.

Here I am, writing to my wife, the love of my life

Then we would get seven or eight letters at once. As it was disconcerting to read the letters out of order, we wrote the letter number on the outside of the envelope. This helped keep them in order when we went to read them.

Here is my wife, Kaye, reading one of my letters

<u>*MAINTENANCE OFFICER*</u>   Due to an unfortunate
series of events, I spent my first 3 years after
commissioning as a Maintenance Officer before attending
Flight School. When I arrived at NKP, the Squadron
Maintenance Officer, for some reason, had to be sent back
to the States. The Squadron Commander pulled another
Officer who had Maintenance experience and myself in and
announced that one of us would be taken off flight status to
serve as the Squadron Maintenance Officer. I was
dumbstruck and disheartened.

If I had to be in Vietnam, I wanted to *fly*, not be a
"ground-pounder". The other guy was a Major and I figured
he could pull rank to get what he wanted.

I spoke up explaining how I had spent time in the enlisted ranks and then as a Maintenance Officer before I got to Flight School and did not want to be denied the opportunity to fly. The Major looked relieved. He said he would gladly take the Maintenance Officer job.

MARRIAGE   The natives we encountered at our Lima sites were a simple, primitive, people who had little contact with other cultures or even each other, due to the extreme difficulty of traveling in the jungle and the harsh nature of their existence, which required nearly all their effort just to survive.

Girls were not a particularly welcome addition to a family. It was felt they ate too much and contributed too little. Frequently, in the remote hill tribes, if a girl was the firstborn, she was killed.

A boy, after all, could learn to hunt and could offer food and protection to the family. In addition, he would not abandon his family at marriage, as a girl did, and would thus theoretically be available to care for the parents as they aged. Also, and most importantly, a boy could be trained to fight for his family and village.

A child of either sex was considered an adult at the age of 12. The boys would marry and build their own hut near to that of their parents. A girl would marry, often as early as the age of 10, and leave the family, sometimes never to be seen again, if her husband lived elsewhere.

Once a year, there was a religious festival, which was held at our overnight site. I was lucky enough to be present and witness one during my tour.

All the fathers from village's miles around would attend with their 10-year old daughters. The unmarried 12-year and older boys and men would attend also. This festival was a combination religious gathering, gossip exchange and marriage-arranging event. On the appointed day, the boys would line the edges of a large pit, perhaps 100 feet across and 10-15 feet deep.

The girls would be put in the center, where they would walk around, wearing their best clothes and as much silver jewelry as their dowry could bear. At a signal, the boys would run to the girl of their choice, grab her and drag her off to the side of the pit, where a Buddhist priest waited to marry them. Often, this was the first time either had met. The girl would most likely not see her former family again due to the difficulties of travel in the jungle.

I saw two boys run toward a particular girl who was wearing lots of silver jewelry as her dowry. They began fighting over her and while they were thus engaged, another boy grabbed her and dragged her off.

If a girl was not taken as a bride at her 10th year, she returned home in shame with her father. She was treated with contempt by the rest of her family until the time for the next festival. If she failed again to acquire a husband at her 11th year, she once again returned home in shame. She then became a virtual slave in the family unit, having lost all rights and affection.

In her 12th year she was taken to the festival for the last time. If she failed for a third time, her father would take her home and tie her to a tree in the jungle as food for the wild animals.

Would-be brides, waiting to be chosen

Waiting for the signal to start

MISSED RESCUE   I have been a member of the
Gideon's since the early 1990's. My involvement, other
than finding a Bible in a motel room, however, dates back to
Vietnam. The Chaplain announced at a Sunday church
service that we had the unique opportunity to purchase
Gideon Bibles and distribute them to the local temples. The
Buddhist priests regarded the Bible as a holy book and
would allow a single copy to be placed in each temple if we
would provide them. A collection was taken up and the
Bibles ordered.

          Obviously, this was not the normal method of
distributing Gideon Bibles. Since the Gideon's could not
visit a war-torn area themselves, we were apparently the
next best thing. When the Bibles arrived and it was time to
distribute them, I was scheduled for alert duty up 'North'. I
found myself torn between two opportunities. I decided to
go on the Bible distribution, reasoning that most of the time
our alerts ended in nothing but a lot of boredom. Therefore,
I traded alert dates with my roommate and went on the
distribution.

          It was a lot of fun; we traveled by sampan through
the jungle on rivers. I saw a lot of the local area and the
interior of some temples I would never have seen
otherwise. When I returned, however, I found that I had
missed a rescue opportunity. When I later stood my
roommate's alert, absolutely nothing happened.

MONEY   There was little money, as we know it,
among the natives. Most everything was accomplished by
barter. People would trade weapons, livestock, and bits of
silver; whatever the market would bear. There were no
banks. The women would string bits of silver together and
wear it around the neck as a sort of necklace. You could tell
at a glance the wealth of a family.

Notice the silver around the neck

MOTION PICTURES   At the overnight site, the CIA had a movie projector and would occasionally show Hollywood films. However we had to view them in a darkened room, with a guard at the door.

     The natives thought the people on the screen were spirits. In addition, their society did not allow touching or kissing except in private between man and wife. If they saw kissing, for example, on the screen, they could not handle it emotionally.

NIGHTTIME SITE

Our overnight site (Lima 20A) was quite different from the daytime one. It was a small city, with a real airstrip capable of handling transport aircraft and was garrisoned with about 5,000 troops. We were able to stay in the CIA compound in rooms with beds.

Unfortunately, the runway dead-ended into a karst or small mountain. This meant that all traffic had to land in one direction and take-off in another, regardless of which direction the wind was blowing.

Everything, other than the runway was dirt, and everything that was dirt was usually mud. This made the runway a favorite gathering place for the locals, who would sit on it and exchange news of the day.

They had to be cleared off the runway before each landing. Fortunately, there was a very simple system to do just that. There _was_ a control tower. The fact that it had no radio really didn't matter, since the people in the tower didn't speak English anyway. Instead of a radio, they had two rifles and two flags. One flag was green and the other was red.

Upon arrival, we would fly down the runway past the tower to see which flag was hanging from the side of the tower. It was always red, meaning unsafe to land. We would fly a wide traffic pattern and pass by the tower a second time. On our second pass, the flag was always green, meaning OK to land. We would fly another circuit and make our landing.

The method used to clear the runway was somewhat unique. When the two men in the tower saw us pass by, they would pick up their rifles and began shooting at the people on the runway! This gave an incentive to clear the runway in a hurry. When all were clear, the men would post the green flag, and we could land.

179

The View from Our Hut at Lima 20A

Some of the Local Children—They Loved Chewing Gum

180

PAINTINGS   I had pictures of my two older boys and my wife painted by a local artist and hung them in my hooch.

The pictures

PARTY SUITS   Somebody got the idea of having 'party' uniforms made up for all the Jolly Green Pilots so we would be more recognizable when we ate in the Club.

Here I am in my 'Party Suit'. Seems sort of stupid now, but it helped pass the time away.

PEOPLE   The natives we encountered while we were at the Lima Sites, lived a hard life and, consequently, did not fool around. They were a very serious people; not given to making jokes, who were quick to take offense and often misunderstood what the Americans were saying or trying to do. Few of them spoke English and they resented anyone trying to get too familiar. Their life and society was a sober, solemn one.

Most Americans who got into trouble did so because they were simply ignorant of the local customs. We were extensively briefed on the more important of these, but the best rule was to simply leave the people alone. None of them had any desire to be a personal 'friend' of a round eyed foreigner.

PICTURES   The natives did not understand modern ways and had never seen a picture before the coming of the white man. They were very superstitious, and when they saw their first picture, reacted strongly. Apparently, their Buddhist beliefs were that the picture stole a part of their soul, or something like that. I had to be very careful when taking a picture, or even carrying a camera, while around them.

PRISON   Discipline was harsh in the military camp. If a native soldier incurred the wrath of his superior, he would be consigned to the local prison. There was no release policy, per se. If he had a wife or family who loved him, they might arrange (bribe) to have him set free. Otherwise, he stayed there until death claimed him, which didn't take long.

The prison was also used to house captured enemy soldiers. We were under strict orders to stay away from it, but I used to sneak over there occasionally. It was nothing more than a large pit, perhaps 20 by 30 feet on the sides and 10-15 feet deep.

The top was covered with the long metal strips used for planking, commonly known as 'PSP'. A small hatch was placed in one corner to allow the prisoners to be put in or taken out.

Other than the prisoners, the pit was empty, with a dirt floor. Due to the near constant rain, the floor was always under about a foot or more of water. Occasionally, when a native Officer was bored, he would come down to the Pit, open the hatch, pull out his pistol and take aim at the prisoners. They would begin a mad stampede to get out of the way, which was difficult to do in knee-deep water. The Officer would shoot one or two and then return to wherever he had come from.

There were no sanitary facilities in the pit; the prisoners would try to squat in one corner to do their business, but the stuff floated around all over. Naturally, the stench was unbearable. The guards would stand upwind, with scarves over their faces. The prisoners all acquired grotesque sores on their bodies due to the unhealthy conditions.

The prisoners were fed the garbage left over from the general camp meal. At feeding time, the guards took special delight in opening the trap door and dangling the food, just above the grasping hands, only to toss it into the muck. The prisoners would grab it as it sank, wipe it off on their dirty clothes, and eat it. It was a sickening sight.

On my last trip to the Pit, as we called it, I was accompanied by a, loud-mouthed, Texan from Dallas. (I must hasten to note that I bear Texans no special grievance, and confess that most are not loud-mouthed, but the stereotype is there, and this man fit it.) He was a co-pilot, and wanted to see the Pit.

Someone told him I had been there and could most likely take him. I hate it when people volunteer me for things I do not want to do. I was not particularly eager to take him, because he was quite unpredictable. But, he was adamant, and I finally gave in. On the way to the Pit, I cautioned him to leave the locals alone. He promised.

When we arrived, there were four guards, spaced out around the Pit. We walked closer, to get a better view. It was jammed nearly shoulder to shoulder with prisoners. I knew there had been a battle just a few days earlier and assumed these were the POW's. One of the guards came up to us.

Before I could say anything, the co-pilot stuck out his hand and said, "Hi! I'm so and so from Dallas, Texas!"

The guard smiled, and began to hold out his weapon.

I said, "Don't take it!"

But it was too late; my Texas 'friend' was holding the weapon.

"Give it back," I hissed.

"I've always wanted to hold an AK-47," he answered.

"I'll let you hold mine. Give it back," I replied.

During this exchange, the guard was smiling, and nodding. He pointed to the co-pilot, then to the Pit, then back to the weapon.

When the co-pilot looked confused, the guard made shooting noises, once again pointed to him, then to the sun and down to the horizon, again making shooting noises.

"What does he want?" asked the co-pilot.

"He's telling you they are going to execute the prisoners when the sun goes down and is offering you a chance to kill one of them now," I replied. "Give the gun back."

"What! Kill the prisoners? No way!" he shouted and slammed the gun into the guard's stomach, doubling him over.

I froze.

The other guards all pointed their rifles at us. We had committed an unpardonable breach of etiquette. In their eyes, we had been offered a great honor. To refuse it, particularly by assaulting the person making the offer, was a grievous insult. I could easily picture us dead.

I put on my best smile and began bowing and "Sa Wat Dee'ing" them. I motioned for him to do likewise and we backed out of their presence, bowing as low as possible.

I do not know why they did not kill us. They certainly had the right to do so in their estimation. That was the last time I visited the Pit.

RESCUE JACKET   Looking for a way to commemorate my rescues, I had a jacket made with the Jolly Green patch on the front and my rescues symbolized on the left sleeve by little men dangling from parachutes for each rescue I had performed, and little parachutes without men for rescues in which I had served as the backup, or 'High', bird. Although difficult to make out in the picture, two of the parachutes had numbers on them to signify a pickup of multiple survivors.

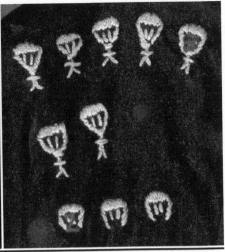

Jacket Front   **Jacket Sleeve**

RETRIBUTION   The Operations Officer was not about to let me get away with ruining his persecution of my roommate, but there was little he could do since I had cleared every step with him before proceeding. I knew I had to step carefully for the rest of my stay, as he would be on the lookout for some way to pay me back.

Our days off between alerts were designed to allow us to relax, and normally we would be left strictly alone. I was perplexed, therefore, when someone came to my quarters quite early in the morning of my day off and told me the Colonel wished to see me.

When I reported to Squadron headquarters in my jungle fatigues, I was told to dress in my class 'B' uniform and return. Although we had them, we never wore our khaki uniforms. I went back to the 'hooch', changed and returned to the headquarters office.

There I sat and cooled my heels until lunchtime, when I was told to go eat and return after lunch. I sat around all day, never able to see the Operations Officer, who was obviously avoiding me.

At the end of the day, I was told I was free to go. A whole day, my one day off, wasted.

The next time I had a day off, the same thing happened. Realizing that this was to be a continuing form of harassment, I made plans for my next day off. I got up early, and walked around behind the 'hooch', near the perimeter of the base for a while, then I returned to my room and went back to sleep.

And that's the way it went, right up to the time of my departure. Every time I had a day off, I would do my disappearing act until whoever was sent to fetch me had left. Then I could enjoy my day. The Operations Officer never spoke directly to me about this, preferring instead, to send others to try to catch me off-guard.

SOUVENIRS   Before I gave up my treks through the jungle, I managed to acquire two handmade flintlock rifles, a crossbow with bolts, several metal weights in the shape of common animals, a portable opium scale, and an ancient bar of silver with the Chinese mintmarks on it.

Getting the flintlocks to the United States required some cunning. I carried them with me when I met my wife and two older boys in Hawaii for my R & R (Rest and Recuperation. A sort of 'vacation' from the war zone.). I wrapped them up and labeled them as "fishing poles". My wife carried them back on the plane. That was before the days of airport scanning!

The weights are quite interesting. Most people in that area could not read or write, but they knew that a rooster, for instance, represented a particular weight. The merchant would place one of the animal weights on one side of a balance scale and then add the grain, or whatever he was selling to the other side until both sides balanced.

The opium scale has an ivory rod with gradation marks carved on it and three strings spaced along the top. The weighing pan is suspended below on strings. To operate it, you place the opium (or whatever you are going to weigh) in the pan and slide a small weight along the rod while holding everything by the appropriate top string until the whole thing balances.

The bar of silver is quite unique. There are Chinese mint mark characters stamped into it. My 'Sandy' friend was researching the mint marks to determine which dynasty they belonged to until we lost him.

THE OPERATIONS OFFICER STRIKES BACK   Cheng Mei was an R & R site in Thailand. Everyone was entitled to a week of relaxation there sometime during their tour. When my turn came, one of the pilots asked me to trade dates with him so he and his buddy could go at the same time.

I traded with him but, when my new time arrived, my nemesis, the new Operations Officer was on the rampage and he refused to let me go. So, I never got my time off or saw Cheng Mei.

TOKYO TRIP   Periodically, someone from our Squadron would be given a permissive temporary duty trip (known as TDY), to Tokyo, Japan. This lucky person would get a day or two in Japan, which was a marvelous place to buy all kinds of stuff, especially electronics.

Other people in the Squadron would beg them to buy things for them, but, generally speaking, unless you were a good friend, you were out of luck as it was a real chore to transport stuff through customs, from one country to another.

Not being one of the 'inner clique', I knew my chances of being picked to go on a trip were non-existent. However, I could think of no reason why I shouldn't go. So I decided to assist in the matter of picking the next person. I went to as many of the people in the Squadron as I could, telling them I was the one going on the next trip, and inviting them to make a list of what they wanted me to bring back for them.

By the time word got back to those in control of such things, I had a long list and a pocketful of money. I was called in 'on the carpet' and dressed down quite severely, but too many people had entrusted me with their money for them to take the trip away from me.

So, I got to see Japan and buy a few things for myself as well as the others. As a side benefit, I discovered that the exchange rate was quite different in Japan than it was in Thailand. This helped defray my expenses.

TRIBESMEN   The mercenary tribesmen who guarded our daytime site were from the Muong (or Hmoung) tribe. They were short, about five feet tall and very proud of their accomplishments. We were cautioned to leave them alone as they had customs that were quite different from ours.

WANDERING IN THE WOODS   Prior to receiving my AK-47 from the mysterious person at NKP, I was determined to acquire one for my use in the event I was shot down.

There were days when the weather was so bad over the North that all the bombing raids were cancelled. If the word came early enough, we would remain at our overnight site, but often we wound up at the daytime site with nothing to do.

On those days I would sometimes go for strolls in the jungle, hoping to run into a friendly native who could supply me with an AK-47. Looking back, I realize those jaunts were incredibly foolish. I had no guarantee I wouldn't run into enemy forces.

I always tried to limit the scope of my wanderings, as I had no desire to become lost. One day I met a man who appeared as surprised to meet me, as I was to see him. We both reached for our weapons and then waited to see what the other was going to do. He spoke no English, but I managed, through gestures, to let him know that I meant him no harm and that I was seeking a weapon.

He gestured for me to follow him, and I did so. We walked for several minutes, always deeper into the jungle. Soon I was quite lost and became rather apprehensive.

Finally, he stopped and pointed to the ground. I realized he wanted me to climb down into a small hole. After a moment's hesitation, I did so, keeping my hand near the gun in my shoulder holster.

When I got to the bottom, I realized I was inside some sort of bunker. There were three other men already there. My 'guide' squeezed in after me, effectively cutting off all hope of escape. Through a small slit, we could view the jungle trail before us.

I was very uptight. There were several weapons in evidence, and I was one against four, if it came to that. I attempted to explain what it was that I wanted. Soon, they produced an ancient, bolt-action rifle, which was cocked and loaded.

This was _not_ what I was looking for, but as I objected, the four became quite angry. Deciding that I had better accept what was being offered, I began to bargain for the thing as if it was what I really wanted. _They_ wanted my pistol. It took agonizing minutes of arguing before they accepted several .38 rounds from my gun belt.

After that, my 'guide' crawled out of the hole and motioned me to follow him. I was never so glad to be out of a situation as I was at that moment. I resolved, if I survived, to make this my last trek in the jungle.

The man, led me back along what appeared to be a different route, then suddenly stopped and pointed off to my right, before disappearing back into the jungle. I realized this was the spot where I had first encountered him. I managed to get back to the alert shack, where the others were curious as to how I had acquired the weapon I was carrying. I told them it was a souvenir. That was my last trip into the jungle.

Back at NKP, I carved out a space in some plastic foam that had been used to ship aircraft rockets and sent the rifle home labeled "Toy Gun".

My wife told me that when it was delivered, part of the end of the foam was broken off and the rifle barrel was exposed. The postman said, "Here is your machine gun," as he handed it to her.

WATCH BAND CALENDARS   This was back in the days of round-dial watches with hands. Someone made small, metal, calendars with tiny tabs that could be bent around the watch band.

My wife got hold of about 10-15 of them and sent them to me each month. I started a watch band calendar contest and soon had people signed up to receive their watch band calendars each month.

Inflight Refueling

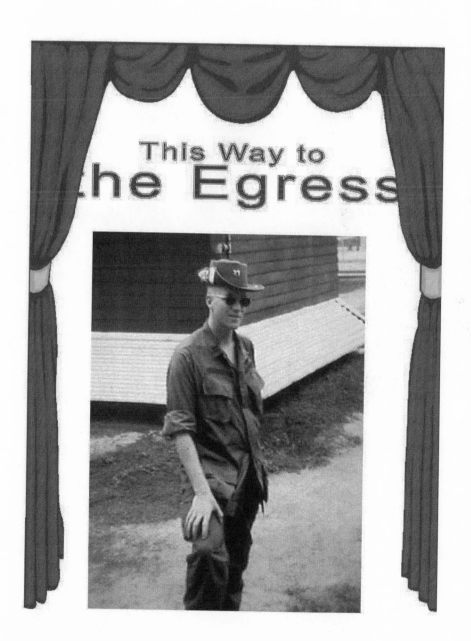

Survivor, being welcomed back by Squadron-mates

This Way to the Egress

I suppose there are many more stories I could relate:

Such as the PJ who hollered, "Where ya goin', Jolly?" as he stood on the ground and watched the helicopter, which was on fire, cut the hoist cable and fly away, only to crash and burn on a hillside. He was the only survivor of the crew.

Or, the Flight Mechanic, who only realized he had put his parachute on over his safety harness, when he was jerked to a stop under the burning helicopter after he had bailed out.

He had to haul himself hand over hand, back up into the helicopter, remove the parachute, remove the safety harness, put the parachute back on, and bail out all over again. All of this took some time. His chute carried him unnoticed over a ridge, where he was picked up the following day. The helicopter, of course, crashed with the RCC inside. The rest of the crew was never heard from again.

Or the survivor, who refused to board a Jolly Green after the pilot, finding the survivor in a large meadow, elected to land instead of hovering.

Not accustomed to retractable gear on a helicopter, the pilot sat it down, gear up, on the belly, crunching several lights on the bottom and rolling around uncontrollably until the he got it back in a hover, lowered the gear, and landed again.

Or the survivor who parachuted out over North Vietnam and lay on the ground, curled up in a ball. In a state of shock, he failed to recognize that rescue was at hand when the helicopter was overhead.

They had to drop the forest penetrator on his head (fortunately, he was wearing his flight helmet) to get his attention!

On and on I could go, but I won't.

Although I was inspired by the 'Streetcar' survivor to undertake this project, I think my prime motivation came from my regret that I do not have any record, and little remembrance, of my father's stories of his various experiences. Because of that, I've left my family, and now others who are interested, these stories about my time in Vietnam.

That's it.

In 2004, the moving Vietnam Wall display was set up in western Kansas, the only point in Kansas that year where it appeared. I was invited to be the keynote speaker at the last day of the exhibition. So, on a Sunday, I found myself addressing a fairly sizable crowd, telling the story of my last rescue. When it was over, various people came forward to thank me and congratulate me on the talk. (Kansas people are *so* nice!)

One woman shook my hand and thanked me profusely. I expressed my gratitude for her words and, in a voice choked with emotion, she said I did not fully understand; she *really* wanted to thank me for what I had said.

She went on to tell me that her husband served in Vietnam at the same time I did. He returned from that experience a changed man, who suffered from nightmares and adamantly refused to discuss what had occurred. Over the years he avoided anything to do with Vietnam, even refusing to attend movies on the subject. This caused her much anguish as she felt he had shut her out of a part of his life.

When she heard that the moving wall display was to be set up near their home, she encouraged him to go and see it. At first, he refused, but on this, the final day, he accompanied her to the event. She said it tugged at her heartstrings as he touched the wall where the names of his dead buddies were engraved.

She wanted to hear me speak, but he refused to attend, saying he said he would wait in the car for her. However, when the event started, he slipped into the stands next to her and said he would stay for only a few minutes.

Instead, he remained throughout my talk, listening intently as large tears rolled down his cheeks while I explained how God had miraculously preserved my life.

When I was done he turned to her with tears still in his eyes and said he felt he was ready to tell her what had happened to him in Vietnam. She began to cry as she talked to me and said she felt that, thanks to me, she finally had her husband back.

As I said, "That's it."

Thanks for reading this.

The Squadron

(Me, in white circle)

Aerial view of NKP

Afterglow...

A "Thank You" to the reader who has stayed with me throughout this narrative...

I would be totally and inexcusably remiss were I to attempt to close this meandering tome if I did not loudly and jubilantly proclaim that, without the divine intervention of my Lord and Savior, Jesus Christ, I would not be here writing these words today.

For reasons of His own, which are still not entirely clear to me, He chose to preserve my life in situations where others were falling.

Whenever I speak on this subject, I invariably get asked three questions:

1   **_"Have I encountered the white light since my time in Vietnam?"_**
The answer, in a word, is "No". That does _not_ mean the Lord has abandoned me. Both Kaye (my wife), and I have experienced many miracles (some that you might doubt the reality of) in the years since; but God, again for reasons of His own, has not seen fit to visibly reveal His protection that surrounds us.

2   **_"Was I scared while I was over there?"_**
Strangely enough, the answer is both "Yes" and "No". Basically, while the dangerous things were going on, I was too busy to be scared. Later, when things had quieted down, I would occasionally experience some retroactive fright, thinking about what I had just been through.

3   ***"Does it bother me to talk about my Vietnam experience?"***

No, not at all. Rescuing someone—realizing that I had saved their life or kept them from captivity, was a very positive experience. Others who served in Vietnam endured a quite different situation.

We now happily reside on the shore of a small, private lake in the state of Kansas, where we have been warmly welcomed and are quite content.

Dave Richardson

You may email your comments to:

vnrescues@xemaps.com

Or visit my website:

www.vnrescues.com

(Lot's of other stuff on the website!)

Jargon

Me—Ready for flight

Jargon

In this section, I have tried to alphabetically list the various terms used in the book which the reader may not be familiar with.

AAA   Anti-Aircraft Artillery

Air Medal 5th ranking U.S. combat award

AK-47   A sub-machine gun of Russian design—the communist equivalent of the M-16

Article 15   One of the lesser forms of Court Martial in the military

Autorotation   A maneuver in which the rotor of a helicopter is disengaged in flight. The weight of the helicopter spins the rotors, allowing a safe landing if done properly.

BDA   Bomb Damage Assessment

Blood Chit   A strip of cloth on which is printed an American Flag and a message in several languages promising to reward anyone who helps the owner

CBU   Cluster Bomb Unit, a hollow casing filled with steel ball bearings packed around an explosive. In some cases, the ball bearings were replaced with tiny, explosive mines.

CIA   Central Intelligence Agency

Cocked   An aircraft which has all its switches set to the "on" position is said to be cocked. One needs merely to apply power to start the aircraft

Crown   The call sign of the orbiting communications relay aircraft used in Vietnam.

DEROS   Date of Estimated Return from Overseas. Generally, one year after arrival.

Distinguished Flying Cross 4th Ranking U.S. combat award

DMZ   Demilitarized Zone, the buffer area that existed between North and South Vietnam.

Drop Tank   A gas tank fitted to an aircraft. It can be jettisoned in flight.

Emergency Beacon A specialized emergency radio which emits a distinctive "beeping" sound on the emergency or "Guard" channel.

FAC Forward Air Controller, a pilot who was familiar with an area flew in a light observation aircraft equipped with smoke rockets, which were used to mark a target for the faster flying jets.

Fast Mover Slang for a jet fighter.

Flak Slang for AAA shell bursts.

Flare-Kicker An enlisted man who stood on the open rear ramp of an aircraft and kicked bundles of flares out at the command of the pilot.

FOD Foreign Object Damage. Jet engines tend to ingest anything that comes close to the intake, causing catastrophic damage.

Fuselage Technical term for the body of the aircraft.

Gomer Slang name for native soldiers.

Ground Clutter Technical term used when describing unwanted radar returns.

Guard Slang for the military emergency radio channel.

Hack Military slang for start timing, or note the time.

High Bird A term for the helicopter which will stand in reserve in the area during a rescue attempt. The idea was that the "Low" helicopter would make the pickup, while the 'High' bird orbited nearby. If the "Low" bird was shot down, which happened occasionally, the "High" bird was expected to immediately fly to the location where the first helicopter had been shot down and rescue everyone. Often, this could be done while the enemy was congratulating themselves over downing the first helicopter. If both helicopters were shot down, which also happened on occasion, two additional helicopters would be launched from the home base. They would fly into the area and start all over again. This process would continue until we ran out of helicopters or everyone was rescued.

Ho Chi Minh Trail	The name given to the network of trails between North and South Vietnam and/or the trails passing through Laos from North to South Vietnam.
Hooch	Slang name for living quarters.
Hover	A maneuver in which the helicopter stays in one spot during flight.
Jink	To fly evasively, in an effort to avoid enemy fire.
Jolly Green	Call sign of the rescue helicopters.
Jungle Penetrator	A heavy, pointed, metal object, about 3 feet long, that was attached to the end of the hoist cable. It had paddles which could be folded down as seats, as well as a safety strap.
Karst	Local name for extremely steep and rocky mountain peaks.
Knot	Slang for Nautical Miles per hour, the counterpoint to MPH, or Miles per hour.
Lead	The title given to the commander of a flight of aircraft.
Letter of Reprimand	A means of punishing a military person without resorting to a Court Martial. Although widely used in the enlisted ranks and considered to be of little consequence, it was recognized as the 'kiss of death' when administered to an Officer.
Lima Site	Code name for the secret sites operated by the CIA in Vietnam.
Low Bird	The opposite of 'High Bird'.
M-16	A sub-machine gun of American design; roughly, the American equivalent of the AK-47.
Mayday	A radio emergency code word .
Medevac	Army term for medical evacuation.
MIG	A class of Russian fighter aircraft.
Muong	An indigenous people who were recruited and armed by the CIA in SEA.
NKP	Initials for Nakon Phanom Royal Thai Airbase, Thailand.

PCS	Air Force term for an assignment involving a permanent change of station.
PDJ	Initials for the Plaines des Jarres, or Plain of Jars, in Laos.
Pickup	Slang term for a rescue.
PJ	A 'Pararecsue Jumper; He was the Medic on rescue helicopters.
PLB	Personal Locator Beacon. A portable Emergency Locator Beacon.
Pop Smoke	Slang term for igniting the smoke flare, the last stage in Identifying and locating the Survivor prior to the pickup.
POW	Prisoner of War.
PSP	Pierced Steel Planking, strips of metal about 18 inches wide and up to 20 feet long, which could be joined together to form a steel matting. It was used for many things, primarily to construct quick, temporary, runways.
Radio, Breaking of	It was vitally important that any pilot who was in danger of being captured break his radio. If he did not, the enemy would wait for another day, then turn the radio on to 'beeper' or automatic mode, tie it to a tree, and attempt to shoot down the helicopters that responded to the distress signal.
RCC	Rescue Crew Commander. The pilot in command of the rescue helicopter.
ROE	Rules of Engagement. These were rules imposed on the Military by the national government. In Vietnam, troops were forbidden to fire on the enemy unless fired on first.
RTB	Return to Base.
Round	Slang for a bullet.
SAC	Strategic Air Command – At that time the name for the bomber portion Of the Air Force.
Sandy	Call sign for the A-1 fighters which supported the rescue helicopters.
SAR	Search and Rescue.

Sa Wat dee The accepted form of greeting. One would fold the hands in a position of prayer under the chin and bow, while saying, "Sa Wat dee, kop." This was an acceptable greeting for arriving and leaving, much as 'aloha' can be used for both in Hawaii. When done properly, it also connoted respect.

SEA Southeast Asia.

Silver Star 3rd ranking U.S. combat award

Smoke Flare A portable smoke bomb, which gave off dense, orange smoke for a short time.

Sponson A metal box attached to each side of the HH-3E, which prevented the helicopter from rolling over when floating on water and provided a cavity into which the main gear retracted.

STOL Short Takeoff and Landing.

Survivor Generic name given to the downed pilot.

TACAN Tactical Aid to Navigation, the standard navigational aid used by pilots.

TDY Air Force term for Temporary Duty, an assignment that was not a permanent change of station (PCS).

Tracer A bullet that flames when fired. Useful for correcting a person's aim.

Translational Lift That point at which the helicopter begins to gain sufficient lift for forward flight.

TUOC Tactical Unit Operations Center, the intelligence section where missions were briefed.

UCMJ Uniform Code of Military Justice.

Yet another Newspaper Publicity Photo, taken after Rescue #7

17064634R00121

Made in the USA
Lexington, KY
23 August 2012